1984

THE GOODBYE PEOPLE

THE
GOODBYE
PEOPLE

A PLAY BY

Herb Gardner

FARRAR, STRAUS AND GIROUX
NEW YORK

Toot, Toot, Tootsie! (Good-bye). Words and music by Gus Kahn, Ernie Erdman,
Dan Russo, and Ted Fiorito. Copyright 1922, renewed 1949, Leo Feist Inc.,
New York, N.Y. Used by permission.
Is It True What They Say About Dixie? by Irving Caesar, Sammy Lerner, and
Gerald Marks. Copyright 1936 Irving Caesar, Inc., renewed 1963. Reprinted by
permission of the publishers, Irving Caesar, Samuel M. Lerner Publications and
Marlong Music Corp.
Yaaka Hula Hickey Dula. Words by E. Ray Goetz and Joe Young; music by Pete
Wendling. Copyright 1916 by Mills Music, Inc., renewed 1944. Used with permis-
sion. All rights reserved, including public performance.
Moonlight Becomes You. By Johnny Burke and Jimmy Van Heusen. Copyright
1942 by Famous Music Corporation, renewed 1970 by Famous Music Corporation.
Used by permission.

Library of Congress Cataloging in Publication Data
Gardner, Herb.
    The goodbye people.
    I. Title.
PS3513.A6333G6   813'.5'4   74-11259

For Marlo and her spirit

THE
GOODBYE
PEOPLE

CHARACTERS
in order of appearance

ARTHUR KORMAN

MAX SILVERMAN

NANCY SCOTT

EDDIE BERGSON

MICHAEL SILVERMAN

MARCUS SOLOWAY

ACT ONE

Before the curtain goes up, we hear about twenty seconds of an old Al Jolson recording of "TOOT, TOOT, TOOTSIE! (GOOD-BYE)." *The sound is loud and clear, but it is obviously a scratchy old record.*

JOLSON'S VOICE

   TOOT, TOOT, TOOTSIE! GOOD-BYE.

   TOOT, TOOT, TOOTSIE, DON'T CRY.

   THE CHOO-CHOO TRAIN THAT TAKES ME

   AWAY FROM YOU,

   NO WORDS CAN TELL HOW SAD IT MAKES ME.

   KISS ME, TOOTSIE, AND THEN,

   DO IT OVER AGAIN.

   WATCH FOR THE MAIL,

   I'LL NEVER FAIL,

   IF YOU DON'T GET A LETTER THEN YOU'LL KNOW I'M IN

     JAIL . . .

The music is joined by the sound of rolling surf, gulls, a winter wind, a distant buoy bell, and then the curtain goes up . . .

SCENE: *The beach at Coney Island. It is late February, a few minutes before dawn. The boardwalk lamps are lit, the surf crashes, the winter wind whistles. The audience is where the ocean would be and the beach angles down toward us. Upstage is a section of boardwalk; a wide wooden stairway leads down from it to the beach at right, disappearing into drifts of sand. Far left are two battered phone booths, back to back under the boardwalk, with sand banked against them like gray snow. Above the boardwalk we can see the open sky, and below it the boardwalk planks drop striped shadows on the sand. Under the boardwalk, to the left of the stairs, is a boarded-up refreshment stand, obviously closed for the winter but old and faded enough to indicate that it has been closed for an even longer time. The front of the stand is about fifteen feet wide; it shows years of being battered by wind and water. Above the stand is an old, faded sign; originally silver letters against a blue background, it is now a mixture of the many colors of age, wear, rust, and strong sun. We can just about make out that the sign says "Max's Hawaiian Ecstasies." At center, a weather-beaten pier extends about four rows into the audience.*

AT RISE: *The Jolson song continues for a few moments . . .*

JOLSON'S VOICE

TOOT, TOOT, TOOTSIE, DON'T CRY,
TOOT, TOOT, TOOTSIE, GOOD-BYE,
GOOD-BYE, TOOTSIE, GOOD-BYE . . .

The music fades into the sound of wind and ocean; the stage is empty for a few moments and then ARTHUR KORMAN *enters, run-*

ning breathlessly along the boardwalk and down the steps. ARTHUR *is about forty, wears a Mackinaw with the hood up and a pair of dark glasses, and is carrying a banjo case and a folded newspaper. He is in a great hurry as though late for an important appointment. He goes quickly into the shadows under the boardwalk, emerging in a moment with a folded beach chair, striped with the colors of summer. Moving quickly down center, he drops everything in the sand, unfolds the beach chair, and sits on the edge of it expectantly, looking anxiously out at the offstage horizon where the audience is. A moment; then he checks his watch; then he looks at a page in the newspaper as though to verify something, nods to himself, and returns to his vigilant pose, leaning forward, his eyes squinting with concentration on the horizon. Another moment and then he jumps up, moves down to the edge of the pier for a closer look at the horizon. He is getting annoyed.*

ARTHUR
[*Quietly*]
  Goddamn *New York Times* . . .
[*Going quickly to phone booths.*]
  Who ya supposed to believe any more? Who ya supposed to trust?
[*Deposits coin, dials angrily, glancing over his shoulder from time to time as though something might suddenly happen on the horizon. Speaks into phone.*]
  Hello, *New York Times*? I think we got a problem. We got a definite problem here. Your Late City Edition says here, page 70, column 3: "February 22; sunrise: 6:41." O.K., well, it's six forty-*eight* right now, and I don't know

what's happening up in *your* neighborhood, lady, but down here we got darkness . . . Well, if you're just the operator, then who's responsible, who's on top of the sunrise situation over there? . . . City Desk? Fine. Lemme speak to them . . . Who's this? Mr. Mallory? Mr. Mallory, look out your window. What do ya see? That's called darkness, Mr. Mallory. That's nighttime you got goin' on out there. My name is Arthur Korman, a regular subscriber to your publication, come at great inconvenience to myself to witness the birth of a new day, come on the B.M.T. in quest of beauty and gettin' my ass froze off in total blackness down here! What the hell're you guys usin' for weather information up there? What're ya, a buncha *gypsies* up there!

[*During these last few lines,* MAX SILVERMAN *has entered from under the boardwalk. A short man, about seventy years old, he wears an overcoat, a fishing hat, and an unlit cigar that appears to be part of his face. He carries a shopping bag from which he takes a folding ruler and begins to measure the front of the old refreshment stand; nodding and murmuring in total agreement with everything* ARTHUR *is saying.* MAX *speaks in a rich, full-bodied, tasty Russian-Jewish accent.*]

MAX

Sure . . . sure . . .

ARTHUR

Great. Beautiful. You're sorry. Meanwhile I'm down here at Coney Island, alone in the dark, and you guys're up there in leather chairs, drinkin' hot coffee and makin' the news up outa your head!

MAX

Sure, that's the story . . .

ARTHUR

Of *course* you wanna hang up on me now. What difference do *I* make, right? You don't need *me* . . .

MAX
[*Measuring.*]
Sure . . . sure . . . they don't need you . . .

ARTHUR

I'm just a victim of your imaginary weather reports, the hell with *me,* right?

MAX
[*Nodding.*]
Sure, the hell with you . . . the hell with *all* of us . . .

ARTHUR

The sunrise, the sunset; that's a responsi*bility,* fella . . .

MAX

A big organization . . . who cares? . . .

ARTHUR
Hello? Hello? Hello, Mallory? . . . They hung up.

MAX
[*Folding his ruler.*]
Sure they hung up. A Mallory will hang up on you.

ARTHUR
[*Seeing this stranger for the first time, but continuing his anger.*]
Goddamn it, goddamn gypsies . . .

MAX
You called them at the wrong time, buddy.
[*Looks at pocket watch.*]
I'll tell you the right time to call them. Never.

ARTHUR
[*Shouting, pointing to horizon.*]
I mean, look at that, will ya!

MAX
[*Shouting.*]
Disgraceful!

ARTHUR
What the hell is *that*?

MAX
Blackness! Blackness and darkness!

ARTHUR

I mean, am I being un*reason*able?

MAX

You're being reasonable! Reasonable and cold and lied to!

ARTHUR

What about the front page here? What about "President Buoyed by Senate Support of Asia Policy"? I don't believe *that either* now!

MAX

He could be sitting around at this moment, not buoyed! What do *we* know? We know what they *tell* us!

ARTHUR

Far as I'm concerned they've thrown a doubt on their entire Late City Edition!

MAX

The *Daily News* too! You can forget *them* also!

ARTHUR

I mean, really, who ya supposed to *trust* any more?

MAX

This city, forget it! It's a miracle even that the telephone worked!

ARTHUR

The goddamn B.M.T., we sat stalled thirty minutes in the tunnel this morning!

MAX

Garbage in the river, smoke in the lungs, and everywhere the Mallorys are hanging up!

ARTHUR

And who do ya *talk* to? What do ya—

MAX

They don't care, they cover up! It's a scientific *fact* that every minute the entire island is gradually sinking into the ocean! Do they *mention* it? Do they *do* anything? Next week we'll all be on Sixth Avenue breathing through *straws*; and nobody *mentions*!

ARTHUR

[*Quieting down; becoming more aware of the stranger he's been talking to.*]

Funny, I'm usually the only one around here at this hour; do you—

MAX

[*Still angry.*]

A big organization, they don't *care*!

[*Close to* ARTHUR, *confidentially*]

I'm last night at Katz's Delicatessen; forty-six tables, what they take in there, one night, unbelievable. It's 1 a.m., two frankfurters, I'm a happy man. Suddenly they're closing up, they say go finish your hot dogs outside; in a flash of an eye I'm on the street. A big store, who needs you? A little store, they let you finish. But do you know who owns a little store these days? I'll tell you who. Nobody. And that's the whole story today. Yessir, that's what you got in your world today. How-do-you-do-sir, Max Silverman right here!

[*Suddenly shoots out his hand.*]

ARTHUR
[*Shaking his hand.*]
Arthur Korman.

MAX
What're ya hangin' around here?

ARTHUR
Well, actually, I've come to see the sunrise . . .

MAX
Sure. Why not? A sunrise is nice. What line are you in? I'll bet you're in the art line.
[ARTHUR *nods.*]
Sure, I figured the art line. Where are you located?
[ARTHUR *hands him a card;* MAX *holds it up close to his eyes.*]
"The Jingle Bell Display Company. Bill Fairchild, Pres-

ident. Arthur Korman, Designer." I'll tell you right now,
I like the sound of the whole organization.

[ARTHUR *sits in beach chair, looks off at horizon.*]

Right, you better get ready. Because a sunrise out here'll
run you, tops, ten, fifteen minutes.

[*Sits next to him on chunk of driftwood.*]

A whole week now I see you here, who knew we could be
such terrific pals? With your odd behavior; what is that to
sleep here in February?

ARTHUR

I don't *sleep* here, Mr. Silverman; sometimes while I'm
waiting for the sunrise I—

MAX

A whole half hour I spoke to you yesterday. With them
dopey glasses, who knew the eyes were closed? I'm having
a gorgeous and terrific conversation, right in the middle
you say, "Goodbye, Bill . . ."

ARTHUR

[*Rises, begins to fold beach chair as though to move on; politely*]

Talked in my sleep, eh? Well, that's—

MAX

A fella comes in February to dream about Bill. Funny
glasses. Goodbye, Bill. Jingle Bells. Arthur, you'll pardon
me, but maybe you're a fairy?

ARTHUR

Mr. Silverman, Bill is my employer's name, I—

MAX

Arthur, you'll be what you want to be, I'm still your pal!
[*Rises, a sympathetic hand on his arm.*]

Listen, you'll make a life for yourself. I'll tell you somebody who doesn't have problems. Nobody.

[*His arm around* ARTHUR, *leading him up center;* ARTHUR *carrying
the chair.*]

O.K., O.K., you're being straight with me, I'll be from the
shoulder with you . . . it's time I revealed to you my true
identity . . .

[*Points to boarded-up stand.*]

You see that sign? That place? "Max's Hawaiian Ecstasies"? Well, that Max from there . . . and this Max . . .
are one in the same Max . . .

[*Turns to him, quietly*]

I am that Max, of Max's Hawaiian Ecstasies . . . Yessir.

[MAX *steps back, waiting for a big reaction to this revelation.*]

ARTHUR

[*Politely*]

Oh . . .

MAX

Of course, we been closed now awhile for various altera-
tions, remodeling, renovations, and modernization . . .

ARTHUR

Uh-huh. How long?

MAX

Twenty-two years. A special place, you gotta wait for the right moment.

ARTHUR

[*Attempting, politely, to disengage himself.*]
Mr. Silverman, I think the sunrise is about to—

MAX

We had here a class operation . . .

ARTHUR

I see a bit of light on the—

MAX

Al Jolson. Yessir, Jolson himself comes once for a frank-furter—*two* frankfurters and a large coconut drink; July 10, 1943, he's here on the boardwalk for a War Bond Rally. Gives you an idea the type clientele.
[*He slaps the side of the stand; the small building shudders with age.*]
We had 'em all here; your various show-business greats, your various underworld personalities, a couple artists, tenors from the opera, some of your top politicos, they come running from all walks of life. You're asking "Why?" and the question will be answered! Because we

had here . . . ecstasy. Grass on the walls, lush; hanging from the ceiling, jungle novelties; tropical foliage; had a record playing with your various exotic-bird noises. A coconut drink costs a dollar. Can you imagine what that was in 1943, a dollar for a soda? Musta been some terrific soda, right? And frankfurters—ground special, my own meat—frankfurters that you could soar to the sky, one bite and you need a pilot's license! Hamburgers I wouldn't even discuss, *tears* would come to your eyes . . .
[ARTHUR *has put down his beach chair, listening.*]
And crowds, crowds all the way back to Tenth Street, on Saturday nights back to Neptune Avenue . . . They ate on the beach here, pineapple paradise under the moonlight, summer nights that last forever . . . and up above the store, with soft blue lights, put a shiver in your neck, my sign, my credo, with silver letters for Silverman, it said, "Without a Little Ecstasy, What's Life? Don't Worry about the Prices!"

ARTHUR
Well, that must've been—

MAX
Unfortunately, they started worrying about the prices . . .
[*Goes to stairway, taking in the whole neighborhood with a sweep of his hand.*]
And the big places started to open on the boardwalk . . .

aluminum nightmares! Fifteen cents for a frankfurter! Coney changes under my feet; comes in garbage, goes out style. Who needs ecstasy? My place becomes here a ghost and haunts itself . . .

[*Moves up the stairs, points lovingly to an area of boardwalk above his store.*]

Was once, right there, Soloway's Bath, Beach, and Sports Club. Guided by the hand of Marcus Soloway, a gentleman and a genius; with columns, pillars, almost marble, rising up. On top, a roof built like a pagoda would make even a Chinaman happy . . . and, oh, oh, on this roof a sea lion, buddy . . . almost marble, with green eyes that looked out at the sea . . .

[*A sweep of his hand; shouting.*]

And now gone! The only Roman Jewish Oriental bathhouse the world will ever know!

[*He sits on the top step of the stairway, for the first time like an old man.* ARTHUR *is at bottom of steps, listening.*]

You want to know who ends up twenty-two years with a job manager of the Burger Circus, cheap food on Lexington Avenue? Me. Max. The same Max. And Marcus Soloway is today a salesman sports goods in Jersey. You want to know God's job? To give every great man a squash!

[*He stands, angrily*]

Yessir, I got *that* boy's number! He's a joker, a fooler, a whimsical fella, and a rascal altogether!

[*Moving down the steps to* ARTHUR.]

What kinda monkey business that without Max to give it

a spin, the world turns anyway? How come the ocean is still there without Soloway's sea lion watching it?
[*Poking* ARTHUR's *chest.*]
I'll tell ya what, mister; the difference between me and God is that I know how to run a class operation.

ARTHUR
Mr. Silverman—

MAX
Would you let me talk, please? I have only recently re-covered from a serious and delicate operation on my only heart—
[*Gives* ARTHUR *a slight shove;* ARTHUR, *off-balance, sits back down on the beach chair.*]
I'm buddies with the angel of death, I'm operating on a very tight schedule, so close-'em-up-the-mouth—

ARTHUR
I'm sorry, I—

MAX
You came here to see the sunrise; but today, mister, Max Silverman *also* rises!
[*Leans close to him.*]
I notice that don't take your breath away . . . but they almost took *mine* away altogether. Two months in Mount Sinai Hospital—all day my family sits around the bed watching me with funerals in their eyes. Every lively move

I make is to them a miracle and a wonder. I lift a cup of tea, I get an ovation. Suddenly I'm a talented man and my talent is that I'm not dead. What I got to look forward is in ten years I'll be my brother Harry whose big accomplishment is that he's eighty years old and he gets outa bed every morning! Look at Harry, they say, will you look at him how he eats his *soup,* look how *cute,* look how he hears almost ten percent of what you say to him—

[*Suddenly, rushing to* ARTHUR.]

And they almost had *me!*

[*Grips* ARTHUR's *arm urgently.*]

I'm lying in the bed there and I'm starting to think I'm terrific just because I'm *breath*ing!

[*As though in the hospital room*]

I look around at them . . . my wife, God bless her, a silly person . . . Joey the Bum and Michael the Bore . . . Rhoda and Barbara . . . or Barbara and Rhoda . . . married to Harold and Arnold . . . or Arnold and Harold . . . A *gross* of grandchildren: Sean, Adam, Kate, Mary-Jane, Mindy, Mandy, Molly; it's an Irish lullaby! "Dad," says Rhodabarbara, "not a *bunch* people—a bunch *of* people—you can hear that, can't you, Dad?" From the whole crowd one person who ain't ashamed—*likes* even how I sound, and that's Shirley, Crazy Shirley. I used to think the whole family isn't a total loss there's one Crazy Shirley in there . . .

[*Shouting.*]

The hell with *her also*! A whole year I don't hear from

her! She run away from her husband—O.K., her used husband with his used-car lot, *him* you run away from—but why from Max? Max who is adorable!

[*Exhausted, leans back against the dune.*]

She wasn't there . . . and in the bed I look around at the rest of them, with their blank faces you could write a message on their foreheads like on a sheet of paper . . . and I'm thinkin', if I die, when I die, this here is all I leave, this is all the world will know of me, this bunch American beauties here . . . so *then,* right *there*—

[*Shoves himself upright off the dune; shouting.*]

—buddy, I make-'em-up my mind—right there in Mount Sinai Hospital, Room 423, semiprivate—I decided *not* to die! Halt! Stop the horses! Rip it from the schedule! Max has got business to do! First I gotta leave something you should know I been around; somethin' says I was alive, somethin' terrific, somethin' classy . . . somethin' beautiful; can't just leave behind this crowd of Silvermans . . .

[*The lights have gone out along the boardwalk; and now the sun begins to rise, throwing a pink glow on the sand and the edges of the boardwalk.*]

. . . and what's it gonna be?! *Yessir*—

[*He points to the boarded-up stand.*]

—rising up from the ashes—fresh, thanks God, like a daisy —awakened like a sleepin' princess—here ya go, whatta ya say—the grand and gala reopening of—the *Original Max's Hawaiian Ecstasies!*

[ARTHUR *murmurs something.*]

I'll tell ya who's not gonna die! *Me;* the original Max!

[ARTHUR *murmurs, shifts in his chair.*]

I'll tell ya—

ARTHUR
[*Murmuring.*]

Goodbye . . . goodbye, Bill . . .

MAX
[*Goes to chair, looks at* ARTHUR; *then lifts up* ARTHUR's *sunglasses.* ARTHUR *is sound asleep.*]

Out like a light. You rotten kid. Well, it's your misfortune, buddy; you missed a lot of terrific conversation.

[MAX *notices the sunrise, now a rich, red-orange glow filling the stage.*]

Stupid, you're missing the sunrise! A spectacle, what you came here to see!

[*Shakes* ARTHUR, *shouting urgently.*]

Wake up! *You're missing it!* Beautiful view, beautiful words . . . you're missing it . . .

[*Sadly; lets go of* ARTHUR's *arm.*]

Oh, you people are always missing it . . .

[MAX *is silent for a moment, quite still; then he shrugs.*]

What the hell; sleep. I can't bother you. I got business.

[*Picks up the shopping bag, starts up the boardwalk steps.*]

Contacts to make. Money to raise. Business.

[*A* GIRL *steps forward from the striped shadows under the boardwalk; she is wheeling a brightly painted bicycle, a foreign-made racer called a Peugeot. The* GIRL *is a thirty-three-year-old who dresses like sixteen: jeans, serape-sweater, beads, little white boots, everything out of place with her adulthood and the February weather.*

MAX *reaches the top of the steps; looks down, sees her.*]

What is it, girlie? What can I do for you?

[*She shakes her head.*]

You're lost?

[*She hesitates; shakes her head again.*]

The bicycle path is over by Ocean Parkway. Now you'll excuse me, I got business . . .

[*He hoists his shopping bag up under his arm, walks left down the boardwalk . . . stops, looks out at the horizon. The sunrise fills the stage with a red-golden glow. He looks up at the sky, angrily*]

A joker, a fooler, a rascal. Also a show-off!

[MAX *exits to the left of the boardwalk, singing as he disappears from sight.*]

TOOT, TOOT, TOOTSIE, GOOD-BYE,

TOOT, TOOT, TOOTSIE, DON'T CRY . . .

GIRL

[*Singing softly.*]

THE CHOO-CHOO TRAIN THAT TAKES ME

AWAY FROM YOU . . .

ARTHUR

[*In his sleep*]

NO WORDS CAN SAY HOW SAD IT MAKES ME . . .

GIRL
[*Smiles; wheels her bike toward* ARTHUR.]
KISS ME, TOOTSIE, AND THEN . . .

ARTHUR
[*After a moment*]
DO IT OVER AGAIN . . .

GIRL
WATCH FOR THE MAIL . . . I'LL NEVER FAIL . . .
[*Silence.*
She moves closer, testing the depth of his sleep.]
WATCH FOR THE MAIL . . . I'LL NEVER FAIL . . .
[*Silence.*
She rings her bicycle bell. Silence; he is deeply asleep. She feels the sunrise on her face; looks out at it; awed, whispering.]
What'd he call ya—Arthur? Arthur, you're missing a beauty . . .
[*Glancing up and down the deserted beach.*]
Oughtta be a bigger crowd for a show like this . . .

ARTHUR
[*Singing.*]
IF YOU DON'T GET A LETTER THEN YOU'LL KNOW
    I'M IN JAIL . . .
[*She laughs. He murmurs.*]
Quitting, Bill . . . leaving organization . . . goodbye, Bill . . .

[*He moves restlessly in his sleep.*]

Light, light . . . shade is up . . .

[*She holds her hand in front of his eyes. He relaxes peacefully.*]

GIRL

[*She lays her bike down near him, sits next to him in the sand; leans against his chair, continuing to hold her hand in front of his eyes.*]

Tell ya what, Arthur . . . altogether, so far, it's the best relationship I've had with a man this year.

[*He murmurs.*]

Nancy. Nancy Scott.

[*He murmurs.*]

Yes, I'm married; but maybe we can work something out.

ARTHUR

Bill . . .

NANCY

Bill will just have to understand. That was never a very healthy relationship, anyway.

[*Leans more comfortably against his chair.*]

Oh, beach buddy, we have got something very valuable here. Dr. Berman says I've got trouble relating to people. Well, he's wrong. I relate terrific. It's when they all start relating *back* at me, *that's* when the—

ARTHUR

Leaving organization, Bill . . .

NANCY

Nobody blames you . . .

ARTHUR

Quitting, Bill. *Had* it . . . Quitting . . .

NANCY

You took as much as you could . . .

ARTHUR

Up to here, Bill. Quitting now . . . no more, goodbye . . .

NANCY
[*Indicates banjo case.*]
   I think it's time you concentrated on your music anyway—
[*A phone rings. She glances about.*]
   Phone. Where?
[*The phone rings again.*]

ARTHUR
[*Cordially, in his sleep*]
   Hello. How are ya?
[*A third ring; she spots the two booths under the boardwalk, runs for them.*]

NANCY

   Jesus, who calls up the beach?
[*Opens door to first booth; grabs phone.*]
   Hello, Atlantic Ocean.

[*Sits down in booth.*]

Huh? Well, who is *this*? . . . Sounds like rolling surf because it *is* rolling surf. Arthur Korman; yeah, just a second—

[*Leans out of booth.*]

Arthur! For you on "one"! Arthur! Phone! Hey, Arthur!

[*He remains motionless.*]

Sorry, he's asleep. That's right, on the beach. Who shall I say called? Oh . . . Bill. Look, Bill, hate to break it to ya like this, but he's quitting. Yeah, leaving the organization. Well, what can I tell ya, Bill, he seems very definite about it. Yeah, O.K., 'bye.

[*She hangs up.*]

ARTHUR

Leaving, Bill . . . leaving . . .

NANCY

You left.

[*She leaves the booth, unaware that* EDDIE BERGSON *has just entered at the top of the boardwalk steps. A tall man, about forty, he wears an overcoat and carries two containers of coffee.* NANCY *looks back at the phone booth, suddenly regretful about what she's done. She moves toward* ARTHUR.]

Mr. Korman . . . I think you better wake up now, I—

EDDIE

Shirl . . . ?

[*She freezes; her back to him.*]
    Shirley . . . ?
[*After a moment, she turns to him.*]
    Oh. Oh, excuse me, miss, I was . . .
[*He is about to leave; he stops, looks at her for a long moment.*]
    Hey . . .
[*He takes a step down the stairs.*]
    Hey, is that you, Shirl?

NANCY

Can you start with an easier question?

EDDIE

Jesus . . . the nose . . .

NANCY

Yeah; how about that?

EDDIE

And you musta lost . . .

NANCY

Twenty pounds. Five in the nose alone.

EDDIE

Your . . . your hair, it's . . .

NANCY

Mr. Gaston calls it "Dazzling Midnight."

EDDIE

Jesus . . .

[*Coming slowly down the steps.*]

I mean, you warned me on the phone, but . . . I was still lookin' for, y'know, Shirley.

NANCY

That makes two of us.

EDDIE

[*At bottom of steps.*]

Well, hello.

NANCY

Hello, Eddie.

ARTHUR

[*Cordially, in his sleep*]

Hello. How are ya?

NANCY

[*Shrugs.*]

I think he's a friend of my father's.

[*Going to dune, far from* ARTHUR.]

Appreciate your coming down here, Eddie. I thought, y'know, a divorce isn't something we should talk about on the phone, right?

[*He nods, following her to dune.*]

I mean, we owe each other a better goodbye than that, don't we?

EDDIE

Yeah. Kinda cold here, though, isn't it?

NANCY

Been coming here a lot this winter . . .
[*Points to Peugeot.*]
The bike keeps me in shape, but I need destinations, see.
And the mornings are lovely here . . .

EDDIE

Yeah. It's very nice. Very cold here, though. Maybe we
could—

NANCY

That was Pop's store there. When I was a kid I used to
come here at this hour to help him cut the French fries . . .
[*With* MAX's *accent*]
"Crispy, curly edges, please!"
[*Looking at the store.*]
Funny, it gets smaller every time I—

EDDIE

Cold. You want my coat?

NANCY

No thanks.
[*Sits.*]
Here; pull up a dune, Eddie.

EDDIE

[*He sits opposite her. They are silent for a moment.*]

Long time, Shirl.

[*She nods.*]

Here. Coffee. I think it's still warm.

[*She accepts one of the containers; nods thank-you.*]

Fact is, I got over here pretty fast. Took a '71 Chevy hard-top off my lot, come over on the Belt Parkway. You take your East Side Drive down to your Brooklyn-Battery Tunnel; then—zing—you shoot right out on the Belt till you hit the Coney Island exit.

[*Silence; they sip their coffee.*]

So what ya been doin' with yourself, Shirl?

NANCY

Been working on television, Eddie. Acting.

EDDIE

No foolin'.

NANCY

Yeah. Me and my new nose. I do that commercial for Wonder Suds where they say, "Did you know washday could be paradise?" I play the girl who didn't know.

EDDIE

Hey, no foolin'.

NANCY

Here, I'll show ya—
[*Flashes a blank, wide-eyed stare.*]
That was me, not knowing.

EDDIE

Great eyes.

NANCY

What?

EDDIE

You still got the same eyes. Great eyes.
[*Silence; they sip their coffee.*]
Does it hurt a lot when they do it—fix up your nose?
[*She shrugs.*]
Yeah, I figured it must hurt a lot. Look, how about you
come back with me, stay married and everything—

NANCY

Eddie—

EDDIE

I got the car right out on Neptune, we could—

NANCY

No, Eddie—

[*Then gently*]
Eddie, we decided; we agreed—

EDDIE
Right.

NANCY
I'm sorry, I—

EDDIE
Right. Right.
[*He sips his coffee.*]

NANCY
Believe me, Eddie, I've thought about it a lot; even been to
an analyst, I—

EDDIE
What does he say?

NANCY
I do most of the talking, he just listens—

EDDIE
Then come home, Shirl, I can do that for ya at home—

NANCY
Eddie—

EDDIE

Jesus, Dazzling Midnight, a new nose, what do ya—

NANCY

"What do ya need it for?" Your favorite question, Eddie; they're gonna put it on your tombstone: "Here Lies Eddie Bergson; What Did He Need It For?"

EDDIE

Fact is, I love you, Shirl . . . and I loved you just the way you were, too . . .

NANCY

Dear, sweet Eddie . . . you were in love with a midget. I'm what I'm asked to be, see, and you were asking for a little toy lady. Eddie, I had to get outa there before I got too short to reach the doorknob . . .
[*Grips his hand urgently.*]
Oh, Eddie, there's so much maybe I can be, so much I want to . . .
[*She looks at him for a moment.*]
Gettin' any of this, Eddie?

EDDIE

Gettin' the sound of it. Sounds like leaving.

NANCY

Oh, Eddie . . . dear, sweet—

EDDIE
[*He stands.*]
That's enough "dear, sweet Eddie" for today. I'm startin'
to take offense at it.
[*Crushes his coffee container, drops it in the sand.*]
Look, Shirl; it's what people do: being married. It's what
there is. Not fantastic, but what there is. Six years we had
no chairs in the dining room because you were waiting for
fantastic ones. You're lookin' for fantastic, Shirl, and there
isn't any. But there *is* the Bergsons, and that knocks me
out. Just seein' it on your driver's license, "Shirley Bergson," just knocks me out.
[*Walking to the stairs.*]
You still got the same eyes but they look frightened to me.
Out in the cold with frightened eyes; you'll forgive the
expression, kid—
[*Turns.*]
—but what do ya need it for?
[*Checks watch.*]
Gotta open the lot by eight . . .
[*Going quickly up the stairs.*]
Probably make it in forty, forty-five minutes. No traffic
comin' out, but goin' back you get your rush traffic building
up on the parkway. Course, I could always just shoot
straight out on the—
[*Stops at top of stairs; turns, looks down at her.*]
This doctor you go to; he just listens, huh?

[*She nods.*]

Uh-huh.

[*He puts his coat collar up.*]

Well, I think you better go to one who talks to you; because, fact is, Shirley, it's really very cold out here.

[*He shoves his hands deep into his coat pockets, turns left down the boardwalk, and exits quickly.*

Silence. There is the sound of a lone and distant buoy bell. A gust of wind; she hugs herself against the cold.]

NANCY

Well; looks like you and me, Art.

ARTHUR

Goodbye . . .

NANCY

These seaside things never last . . .

[*Going to her bike.*]

Listen, Arthur, we tried, we hoped . . . but let's be sensible; it's over. I think the best thing is a simple "goodbye" . . .

ARTHUR

Goodbye . . .

NANCY

Never really felt like a woman with you, anyway. I think it had a lot to do with your calling me Bill all the time . . .

[*She suddenly lets go of her bike, buries her face in her hands, trembling. The bike falls over in the sand. After a moment she looks up, frightened, surprised by her own behavior.*]

Goddamn it . . .

[*She marches angrily to the two phone booths, enters one of them, deposits coin, dialing fiercely. A gust of wind: she shivers; speaks into phone.*]

Hello, Dr. Berman? Nancy Scott. Look, I'm sorry to bother you at this hour, but I want my money back. It's not working out, Berman; I asked you for happy and fulfilled and you gave me lonely and frightened.

[*Sits in booth, shivering.*]

Listen, I . . . I think Nancy Shirley Silverman Scott has gone and flunked the freedom test. The alone thing . . . I can't seem to handle the alone thing. It's not the dark I'm afraid of; it's the light, it's the mornings, it's the goddamn mornings. I wake up next to lovers with noses as strange to me as my own. I know they must be lovers because they never look like friends. Maybe I should go back to Eddie, huh? I mean, he's still got the same face . . .

[*Quietly; hugging herself against the cold.*]

Listen, keep the money; just give me an estimate—I'm thirty-three, how many years are gonna be left by the time I figure out how to live them? Make me happy, Wizard; make me happy and we still got a deal . . . a happy above happy that guilty can't reach; a happy so high that the guilties'll die on their way up after me . . . Hello? Hello? . . . God damn you, *wake up*! Everybody *up*!

[*She stands, shouting into the phone.*]

I don't care *how* early it is! Don't you know a crazy lady when you hear one? O.K., Berman, that's it. We've *had* it. We're finished! You *bet* I'm serious. Goodbye; I don't need you any more. I don't need you . . . So I'll see you at two o'clock, O.K.? Boy, are you lucky I can't make a decision.

[*Hangs up sharply. Quietly, to* ARTHUR]

Problem now is what to do till two o'clock.

[*Going to her bike, which lies in the sand next to* ARTHUR'*s chair.*]

This is the difficult period, see: between doctor's appointments.

[*Settles herself down in the sand between the chair and the bike.*]

Pop'll be back. I'll wait for Pop . . .

[*Rests her head against the bike.*]

No sleep all night . . .

[*Closes her eyes.* ARTHUR *suddenly moves in his sleep—she whispers urgently.*]

No, no, don't go . . .

[*He relaxes again, murmuring peacefully.*]

Good. Tell ya the truth, I hate to sleep alone . . .

[*Closes her eyes, drowsily*]

Just don't wake up, see . . . As long as you don't wake up, m'friend, you are the best there is . . .

[*Her voice trailing off.*]

Hey, don't feel the wind down here . . . no wind, the best . . . the best . . .

[*She is asleep.*

Silence.

ARTHUR *awakens; he stares out at the horizon for a few moments, trying to remember where he is. He looks down sleepily, sees the bicycle wheel; he studies it curiously for a few moments— suddenly startled to see a pair of feet next to the wheel and an entire girl connected to them.*]

ARTHUR
Oh . . .

NANCY
[*Opens her eyes, also startled.*]
Oh . . .

ARTHUR
Hello. Hello there . . .

NANCY
Arthur, you're awake.

ARTHUR
Yes. Yes, I am. Yes.

NANCY
[*Rising.*]
Hello.

ARTHUR
Hello. How are ya?

[*Rising.*]
Good morning.
[*Stumbling over the bicycle.*]
Your bike?

NANCY
Yes.

ARTHUR
Nice bike.

NANCY
Ten-speed Peugeot with handle brakes.

ARTHUR
Hey, the old guy . . . the old guy, Silverman; where's—?

NANCY
It's a curse. All night long I'm an old Jewish man and in the morning I turn into the beautiful girl you see before you.

ARTHUR
[*To horizon*]
Oh, God. Oh, my God—

NANCY
What—

ARTHUR

The sun! Looka that! It's up! It's up already! Goddamn
sunrise, they slipped another one right past me . . .
[*Slumps defeated in beach chair.*]
Looka that. Six mornings in a row . . .
[*Jumps out of his chair.*]
Excuse me. You wanna sit down? Forget it, stranger on
the beach; who knows, right? I don't blame you. I'm
Arthur Korman, I'm harmless, how-are-ya?
[*Holds out his hand—withdraws it before she can respond.*]
Right. Watch out, I could be anybody. A nut. This city; I
know how you feel.
[*She sits down on the beach chair.*]
Beautiful. Look, you sat down. I'm Arthur Korman; I'm
completely, completely harmless.
[*Shakes her hand vigorously.*]
Don't worry about it. You're free to leave any time. You're
a very pretty girl. Exceptional.

NANCY

Thank you, I—

ARTHUR

Don't worry about it.
[*Sits opposite her, on sand dune.*]
I'm just going to sit here and you sit there and everything'll
be beautiful. You want some coffee?

NANCY
Great; yes.

ARTHUR
Oh; I don't have any. How did you know my name? You must be freezing. Hey, I'll give you my coat.

NANCY
Truth is, I am cold, if it isn't—

ARTHUR
Beautiful. Beautiful.
[*Taking off his coat.*]
Situation like this, believe me; you know how to handle yourself. May I ask your name?

NANCY
Nancy Scott.

ARTHUR
Beautiful. I like the way you handle yourself.
[*He has forgotten to give her the coat.*]

NANCY
Excuse me . . .

ARTHUR
Right, baby.

NANCY

Your coat, I—

ARTHUR

Oh, my God, of course—
[*Rolls it up, tosses it to her like a basketball.*]

NANCY

Thank you.

ARTHUR

So what're ya doin' around here? I come to see the sunrise, but I fall asleep.

NANCY

Don't worry; great thing about the sun is that it comes back every morning.

ARTHUR

Even fell asleep on this crazy old guy today . . .

NANCY

He's my father.

ARTHUR

Weather like this, how come you don't wear a coat or something?

NANCY

That crazy old guy, he's my—

ARTHUR

I mean, it's February.

NANCY

Well, when I go to buy coats I think I'm very tall. I've got six tall coats and they all look terrible on me.

ARTHUR

Beautiful.

NANCY

So if I was tall I'd be warm. Meanwhile I'm short and cold.

ARTHUR

Beautiful. Beautiful. See what we're doing? We're talking. Opening up. This is terrific.
[*After a moment*]
You got to let it happen. Letting it happen is what it's all about.
[*Silence; he picks up his banjo case, opens it, takes out banjo.*]
This is called a Whyte Lady, this banjo. Great sound. Haven't made 'em for thirty, thirty-five years.
[*Sits next to her on chunk of driftwood, holding the banjo with great affection.*]
See this here; carved bone pegs . . . pearl inlay on the frets . . .

NANCY

Would you play something for me?
[*He holds the banjo in playing position; plucks one of the strings,
listens to it critically, tightens it. Silence for a moment. He puts
it back in the case.*]

ARTHUR

Tell ya what, it wouldn't be a good idea.

NANCY

Why not?

ARTHUR

Because I don't play the banjo.

NANCY

What are you doing with it?

ARTHUR

Carrying it. I carry it.

NANCY

Oh.

ARTHUR

I carry things. Idea is you carry something around long
enough you become obligated to it, see; to learn what to
do with it. Got the instruction book in there too. And my
sculpture tools. Used to do sculpture and I'd like to get

back to it, so I carry my tools in there and it reminds me.
Of my obligation.
[*He snaps the case shut. He looks off at the horizon for a few moments; sings softly to himself.*]

IF YOU DON'T GET A LETTER THEN YOU'LL KNOW

I'M IN JAIL . . .

[*Silence.*]

Well; 'bye now.

[*Rises; picks up banjo case.*]

Yessir, that ol' clock really ticks away, doesn't it?

[*Shaking her hand vigorously.*]

This was great. Talking to you. Beautiful to meet you. Beautiful experience here.

[*Walking briskly to the stairs.*]

Right; but now it's time to start the ol' day goin', huh?

NANCY

Your . . . your coat, I . . .

ARTHUR

[*Going up the stairs.*]

Keep the coat. It's your coat. I want you to have it; it's February.

NANCY

[*Unbuttoning the Mackinaw.*]

Take your coat. I don't want it . . .

ARTHUR
[*At the top of the stairs; he turns to her.*]
  Please. Please keep it . . .

NANCY
[*Holding the coat out to him.*]
  I really don't want it. Here . . .

ARTHUR
[*A casual wave of his hand.*]
  Hey, keep the coat . . .
[*Suddenly, desperately, clutching the banjo case.*]
  Please . . . Keep it . . . Keep the goddamn coat, will ya?
Lady, I gotta leave now. The gaps. The gaps in the con-
versation. The gaps are coming! Get out while you can!
Believe me, you're in for a losing experience. That's it,
lady; that's all I do. You've just seen everything I do. That
was it. I don't follow up with anything. I'd like to play
you a song on my banjo or invite you for a swim but I
don't play I just carry and it's too cold. Forgive me, I'm
sorry; goodbye—
[*He starts to exit left down the boardwalk.*]

NANCY
[*Shouting.*]
  This is a four-thousand-dollar nose!
[*Throws his coat down on the sand.*]
  You're walkin' out on a four-thousand-dollar nose here,
dummy!

[*He turns, startled by her outburst.*]

Don't stand there! Go away! Alla you! I don't need *any* of you! This is Dr. Graham's nose! A top nose! This is Mr. Gaston's hair! Mr. Gaston of Lexington Avenue! This is my agent's name and this is Dr. Berman's attitude and this voice I'm talking to you with is from Madame Grenier, the vocal coach! I'm not just a pretty girl, I'm a *crowd* of pretty girl! A convention . . . a parade . . . a . . .

[*There are tears in her eyes. She turns away from him, sits down on the beach chair.*]

So who needs you; I got company . . .

[*She hugs herself against the cold, trembling.*]

Go away, goodbye; we're goin' over great here . . . Graham, Gaston, Berman, my agent, the madame and me . . .

[*Silence. A gust of wind.*]

ARTHUR
[*Gently*]

Lady, I . . .

NANCY

You still here?

[*She remains seated with her back to him.*]

ARTHUR

Listen, all those people . . . I want you to know something, they did a terrific job on ya.

[*Silence.*]

You really look . . . fine. Just fine.

[*Silence; he comes down the stairs, picks up his coat, stands behind her.*]

Here. You're shivering. Please take this . . .

[*She does not respond; he drapes the coat very delicately over her shoulders.*]

When it gets windy you can put the hood up, O.K.?

[*She reaches behind her head, letting her longish hair fall outside the coat. He assists her carefully with a strand or two.*]

Very real; the hair . . .

[*She continues to look the other way. He touches her shoulder gently.*]

I'm sorry that I upset you. You mustn't take it personally . . . Believe me, you're a pretty girl. You must be a pretty girl because I can't talk to you. I can't talk to you people . . . There's a special code. Some guys know the code. I don't know the code . . .

[*Silence.*]

Please, give me your number. I'll call you. I'm terrific on the telephone.

[*No reply. He shrugs sadly, turns to leave.*]

I know I could have a great life if there was just some way to phone it all in.

[*Starts to walk slowly away.*]

NANCY

[*Quietly*]

The hair, y'know . . . the hair *is* real.

[*He stops, delighted to hear her voice.*]

ARTHUR

I thought so. It had to be.

NANCY

It's just the color that was changed, see.

ARTHUR

Well, it's very suitable.

NANCY
[*After a moment*]
Thank you.

ARTHUR

I think it's *all* very suitable.

NANCY

Thank you.
[*After a moment*]
It's just the nose, actually, that's not mine.

ARTHUR

Really? It certainly *looks* like—

NANCY

I know it's not mine because yesterday at Bloomingdale's I saw another girl with it. Dr. Graham, he does a certain style of nose and it turns out there's a goddamn *army* of us walking around New York with it.

[*They both laugh at this for a moment. She turns toward him.*]
Yukon five, six, one, four, one.

ARTHUR
What?

NANCY
That's my number. For when you're feeling terrific.

ARTHUR
Thank you.

NANCY
Or if you ever want to visit your coat.

ARTHUR
Coats . . .
[*Looks up at the sky.*]
Tall coats, you've got six of them . . .

NANCY
Yes, I—

ARTHUR
The old guy . . . the old guy, you said he was your
father . . .

NANCY
I thought you didn't hear that.

ARTHUR
I didn't. I just heard it now. It takes about twenty minutes for sound to reach me . . .
[*She laughs, enjoying him.*]
See what you're doing? You're listening. How do ya do that? You even look like you're listening. That's the hard part. I gotta work so hard on that part I can't hear a thing . . . there's one now . . .

NANCY
What?

ARTHUR
A gap. And that's just the beginning, that was just a little one—

NANCY
Hey, Arthur—

ARTHUR
Wait'll the big ones come, they can kill ya—

NANCY
Take it easy, we've got plenty to talk about—

ARTHUR
Seems like we've covered everything—

NANCY

About me being pretty, we could talk about that some more. That's always good for a coupla minutes . . .
[*He smiles, relaxing a bit.*]
What's really fascinating, see, is that nobody seems to know me any more . . .
[*He sits opposite her, nodding attentively.*]
My own father, for example . . . Truth is, I was afraid to introduce myself to him. Sees my new nose, hears my new name—I'll wake up at the bottom of the Atlantic with fifty pounds of frankfurter tied to my foot.
[*He continues nodding.*]
You hear any of that, Art?

ARTHUR

Parts. Parts of it . . .
[*Silence. He glances about anxiously.*]

NANCY

Chrissake, that was a *pause*. Pauses are O.K. . . .
[*Another silence. They both glance about anxiously.*]
Uh . . . work—our work, let's talk about our work—

ARTHUR

O.K.—

ARTHUR and NANCY
What kind of—

NANCY

You're first, Arthur . . .

ARTHUR

Well, I've got this sorta silly job . . . I'm with the Jingle
Bell Display Company, see; I run this department there
called Santa's Workshop . . .

NANCY

[*Suddenly, remembering.*]
Jesus, your *job*—

ARTHUR

I *told* you it was silly—

NANCY

Arthur, do you . . . how do you like it there?

ARTHUR

Eighteen years of Christmas? It's a nightmare. I'm slowly
turning into an elf . . .
[*Pacing in the sand.*]
Pixie, pixies. I'm a fella lives with pixies. You hang around
with pixies too long, something happens to your head . . .
Planning to quit any day now.

NANCY

How about today?

ARTHUR
Today?

NANCY
[*A bit of strained laughter.*]
Arthur, this funny thing happened . . .
[*After a moment*]
A nutty, impulsive, funny sorta . . .
[*Turning away, quietly*]
Arthur, forgive me . . . I had no right, I . . .

ARTHUR
[*Gently*]
What is it? Tell me . . .

NANCY
See, this guy Bill called . . .

ARTHUR
Bill, right . . .

NANCY
And you seemed so definite there . . . in your sleep . . .

ARTHUR
Definite in my sleep, right . . .

NANCY
So I told him you were quitting . . .

ARTHUR

Quitting, right . . .

NANCY

Arthur, I'm sorry . . . I was in a crazy mood, I—

ARTHUR

Is *that* what's worrying you? Is *that* what you're worried about? Quitting my *job*? That dumb, silly *job*? I was going to quit *any*way! I was *going* to quit! Not right *now* maybe, not this very *minute;* but I was going to quit! *I was going to quit!* He thought you were kidding, he thought you were crazy, right? Some nut making a joke, right?

NANCY

He *must* have, Arthur, he—

ARTHUR

Eighteen years of my *life,* he couldn't've just—

NANCY

Arthur, he said he'd call *back,* he—

ARTHUR

When? When?

NANCY

In a little while, he—

[ARTHUR *collapses into his beach chair.*]

ARTHUR

[*After a moment, quietly*]

Good. Good. That's nice . . .

[*Recovering, with a grand sweep of his hand.*]

Style, see . . . it's just that I meant to leave with a little
style. Eighteen years, you don't just walk out and slam the
door, right?

NANCY

Of course not.

ARTHUR

[*Opens banjo case, takes out stack of letters.*]

Wrote him twenty-six really fine letters of resignation this
year; it's just a matter of selection . . .

[*Looks fondly through letters.*]

Been working on my style. Even got one here in sonnet
form . . . listen; ends with—

[*Reading, lyrically*]

"The blossom is fruitless for he who seeks the lotus
And I, Arthur Korman, give you two weeks' notice."

[*Rises, points to horizon.*]

Said in the *Times*, "Sunrise: 6:41," so I sent Bill a telegram
with the number here to call me twenty minutes later. I
figured all that beauty comin' up . . . and I would quit so
great. The world being born again; the world and me . . .

[*Smacks his fist into the side of the dune.*]

Damn it, lady, you want a great life, you gotta have like
that book, *Great Whattayacallits,* first!

NANCY

Expectations.

ARTHUR

Right! That's why I started coming here, I got up last Wednesday and I noticed I didn't have any. It was my birthday, forty-one years old and I wasn't even expecting *that* . . .

NANCY

Come on, forty-one's not old . . .

ARTHUR

I know; but it happened the day after I was twenty-three, so naturally I was a little shocked. Wednesday morning— zappo—forty-one. I felt like I'd left a wake-up call for thirty and I musta slept right through it . . .
[*Turns to her, urgently*]
Something terrific was supposed to happen by now, see— some terrific reason for shaving and buying shoes and keeping the clocks wound—something terrific, a dazzler, a show of lights, a—
[*Grips her arm.*]
I had this whole other fella in mind once, lady. You woulda been crazy about him. I was gonna be a sculptor, I had in my mind once . . .
[*His voice trails off; he turns away.*]

NANCY

What, Arthur? Tell me . . .

ARTHUR

Monuments . . . I had in my mind once, monuments.
How do ya like that?

NANCY

Sounds wonderful . . .

ARTHUR
[*His spirits soar.*]
I wanted to sculpt those heroes like you see in the park,
guys on horses with swords, terrific guys outa bronze and
metal and they stay there in the park forever . . . forever,
lady . . .
[*Running to the top of the dune.*]
They got bronze eyes looking outa their heads and bronze
fingers pointing somewheres in particular, and if it's a good
statue, a really great one, you can see five hundred people
in the air behind the guy, looking where his eyes are looking and ready to go where his finger is pointing . . .

NANCY

Wonderful . . .

ARTHUR

So I went to this school to study sculpture . . . Trouble
is, I was in that school for five years and by the time I came
out they were all outa them.

NANCY

All outa what?

ARTHUR

Heroes and parks. They were all outa them. Seems like the world run outa heroes and the parks run outa space and I come outa school all at the same time . . .

[*Slides to bottom of dune.*]

I mean, there just didn't seem to be any call for what I did. Truth is, there's not a helluva lot of action in the monument field . . .

[*Picks up the letters of resignation.*]

So I took this job meanwhile . . . eighteen years of meanwhile and every year they give you a birthday party . . .

[*Going to end of pier, carrying the letters.*]

Except Wednesday it was special; besides the beer there was champagne in paper cups because I been there longer than anybody . . . Everybody singing "Happy Birthday" . . . Bill, the fellas, the secretaries, everybody around me in a circle singing, and all of a sudden I couldn't remember what I'd meant to do with it . . . my, y'know, life. Stood there trying to remember and they went on singing like a machine I couldn't stop, "Happy birthday," they're singing, "happy birthday, dear Arthur," and I wanted to rip the building down, *hit* something, *crush* something, and then I thought I was crying but it turned out I'd squirted champagne in my face from squeezing the paper cup.

[*Suddenly, violently, he crushes the letters in his hands. He whispers.*]

What am I waiting for?

[*Turns to her, shouting.*]

Hey, lady, what am I waiting for?

[*Points to phone booth.*]

Today . . . today I get out! When he calls back, I get out! When he calls back, I *quit*! Not another day dying alive! Arthur says goodbye!

[*He tosses the letters high up over his head.*]

Santa's little helper says goodbye!

[*The letters spin in the air like confetti;* NANCY *bursts into applause.*]

A week late, but here's my birthday and you're at the party!

NANCY

Happy birthday!

ARTHUR

Thank you, thank you—

NANCY

And many happy returns—

ARTHUR

And how about *that*—?

NANCY

What—?

ARTHUR
   No gaps!
[*He races across the beach to her, grips her hands in delight. She laughs, kisses him spontaneously on the cheek.*]
   My God, things are going well here . . .
[*The phone rings.*
   A moment; then he lets go of her hands . . . starts across the beach to the phone booth. She picks up the banjo, roughly plucking the notes for "Happy Birthday" as he marches to the booth, opens the door . . . He puts his hand on the phone, she smiles expectantly . . . he does not pick up the phone; he stands in the booth with his hand on the phone while it continues to ring . . .]

NANCY
[*Quietly, putting down the banjo.*]
   Arthur . . .
[*The phone continues to ring; she shouts urgently.*]
   Arthur! *Arthur!*

ARTHUR
[*He sits in the booth; very quietly*]
   Damn cold here, isn't it . . . ?

NANCY
[*Coming toward him.*]
   Arthur—answer it—

ARTHUR
[*Turning away.*]
   The sunrise—I missed the sunrise . . .

NANCY

I saw it, it was gorgeous, now answer the goddamn *phone*—
[*Shouting above the phone.*]
Arthur, you're using the sunrise as a *crutch*—

ARTHUR

[*Shouting.*]
I know, but I'm a cripple, so it's O.K.—

NANCY

Arthur, you said not another *day*—
[*She grips his arm.*]
You said you were dying alive—

ARTHUR

[*Leaves booth, moving away from her.*]
That listening you do, it has some terrible disadvantages—

NANCY

O.K., go ahead, run away from the truth—

ARTHUR

The truth! The goddamn *truth*! They keep tellin' ya how beautiful it is and they never tell ya what the hell to *do* with it—
[*Shouts at the ringing phone.*]
Stop! Stop! My God, will ya please *stop*—

[*He runs to the booth, slams the door, stands with his back against it; shouts to her above the muffled but insistent ringing.*]

Here's the truth, lady! Ain't it gorgeous? It's eight o'clock. At eight o'clock I go to work. At seven thirty I dream, and at eight o'clock I go to work . . .

[*The ringing stops.*

His back against the booth, he slides down, sitting in the sand; bows his head.]

You see the truth comin', take my advice—run home, lock your doors, paint your mirrors black. The son of a bitch'll kill ya . . .

NANCY

[*Moving toward him.*]

Oh, baby, you're a wailer . . .

ARTHUR

Right. Also a coward and a—

NANCY

[*She kneels next to him in the sand.*]

Arthur, people can change their whole lives; I believe that . . . their whole lives if they want to . . .

ARTHUR

Don't you get it, lady? I blew my time. I used up my turn. My cool talk and my kid's clothes, it doesn't work. Only young is young and they don't let you do it again . . .

NANCY
Arthur, it's—

ARTHUR
[*Nodding sympathetically.*]
I see you got the same kinda problem . . .

NANCY
Huh?

ARTHUR
Excuse me, but I couldn't help noticing the funny clothes . . .

NANCY
What funny clothes?

ARTHUR
The funny clothes you got on . . . the kid's clothes . . .

NANCY
Wait a second, buster—

ARTHUR
I mean, you must be what now: thirty-one, thirty-two?

NANCY
Arthur, you're a charmer . . .

ARTHUR

Forgive me, Nancy . . . it's just I've been the route, I can save you some pain . . .

[*Gently, touching her arm.*]

There's things we can't change. Believe me, they ain't lettin' either of us into the world at half-fare any more. Keep telling yourself you're a kid and—

[*She rises; starts to take his coat off.*]

Hey, what're ya doin' . . . ?

NANCY

Giving your coat back.

ARTHUR

Hey, what're ya doin'?

NANCY

It's called "leaving." You will recognize it by how I won't be here any more.

[*She drops his coat in the sand.*]

ARTHUR

Hey, where ya goin'?

NANCY

[*Lifting up her bicycle.*]

I'm taking my funny clothes and getting the hell outa here.

ARTHUR
[*Scrambling to his feet.*]
Hey, I . . . I alienated you, right?

NANCY
Alienated? I came here a cute girl and I'm leaving a nervous old lady!

ARTHUR
See, it's just . . . I thought we had this problem in common, I—

NANCY
The only thing we got in common is sand in our shoes!
[*Wheeling her bike to the left under the boardwalk.*]
I'm not climbing into any cookie jars with you, buster!
Too late, years passing, that's all you talk about! It's like
hangin' around with the Hunchback of Notre Dame—he
doesn't have much to say, but you always know what time
it is!
[*Gets onto her bike, turns to him.*]
Mister, I'm sorry; but I have looked inside your head this
morning and it's fulla bluebirds. Unfortunately, not one
of them is the bluebird of happiness . . .
[*Starts to ride to the left under the boardwalk.*]
And for your information, I happen to be twenty-six . . .

MAX'S VOICE
[*Approaching, off left; singing.*]
   IS IT TRUE, WHAT DEY SAY ABOUT DIXIE,
   DOES DE SUN REALLY SHINE ALL DE TIME . . . ?
[*She immediately stops, gets off her bike, starts wheeling it in the opposite direction.*]

ARTHUR
   Nancy, you've come back—

NANCY
   I haven't come back, you idiot! My God, I'm surrounded by crazy old men!
[*She starts to drag her bicycle up the boardwalk steps.*]

MAX'S VOICE
[*Coming closer, at left on boardwalk.*]
   DO DE SWEET MAGNOLIAS BLOSSOM
   AT EVER'BODY'S DOOR . . .

NANCY
   Where the hell is he *coming* from—?
[*Turns around, dragging her bike back down the steps, wheeling it to the right under the boardwalk, away from the voice.*]

MAX'S VOICE
[*Coming closer.*]
   AND DO DE FOLKS KEEP EATIN' POSSUM,
   TILL DEY CAIN'T EAT NO MO' . . . ?

IS IT TRUE, WHAT DEY SAY ABOUT SWANEE,

IS A DREAM, BY DAT STREAM, SO SUBLIME . . . ?

[*She stops; deciding to face him, wheels her bike back to the bottom of the stairs, stands there with it proudly as though with her gallant steed, awaiting* MAX.]

DO DEY LAUGH, DO DEY LOVE,

LIKE DEY SAY IN EVERY SONG . . . ?

[*She abruptly lets go of the bike; grabs up* ARTHUR's *coat from the sand, puts it on, zipping the hood up over her head so that only her eyes are exposed; returns to her proud position at the bottom of the stairs.*]

WELL, IF DEY DO, THEN YESSIR,

DAT'S WHERE I BELONG . . .

ARTHUR

The old guy . . .

[*Looks up at the sky.*]

. . . your father, he doesn't recognize you . . . you didn't introduce yourself . . .

NANCY

[*Introducing* ARTHUR *to an unseen audience.*]

Here he is, ladies and gentlemen; Mister Memory . . .

[*Shouting from inside the hood.*]

Chrissakes, go *away*! Please go *away*!

[MAX *appears on the boardwalk, singing with great gusto. Caught up in the finish of the song, he proceeds down the steps like a vaudeville performer, one at a time; and once, for effect, moving back up a few steps before proceeding down for the finish of*

*the song. This performance is not necessarily for anyone's benefit;
it's something he would do even if the beach were empty.*]

MAX
[*Singing.*]
   DO DEY LAUGH, DO DEY LOVE,
   LIKE DEY SAY IN EVERY SONG?
   WELL, IF DEY DO, THEN YESSIR . . .
[*Going for a big finish.*]
   DAT'S WHERE I BELOOOOOONG . . .
[*He takes off his hat and bows to no one in particular.*]

ARTHUR
[*After a moment*]
   Uh . . . very nice.

MAX
   Nice? Nice? What's wrong with wonderful? That's a
song, sir. With a melody. Who since Jolson? Who? No-
body is who. Since Jolson, a wasteland of pipsqueaks.
[MAX *breaks into a warm smile, comes down the steps toward*
ARTHUR, *his arms outstretched.* NANCY *turns to him as he ap-
proaches, takes the hood off.* MAX *passes* NANCY *without any sign
of recognition; goes to* ARTHUR, *grips his shoulders in greeting.*]
   Arthur, my sleeper, my darling, you're awake; terrific!
   I see you and my heart, what's left of it, skips a beat.
[*Indicating* NANCY.]
   Good. Good. You got yourself a girl friend.

[*Moving down to pier, his arm around* ARTHUR, *confidentially*]
What happened, it's all finished with Bill? Good.
[NANCY *sits on the bottom step of the stairway, zips up her hood.*]
You got yourself a shy one. Do me a favor, you got a match?
[*Indicates his cigar;* ARTHUR *lights it.*]
Good. Now one more thing I need from you. Ten thousand dollars.

ARTHUR
Huh?

MAX
I'm lookin' for who's gonna get in on the ground floor, get a nice percentage of Max's Hawaiian Ecstasies. Who's gonna be the lucky fella? Two days now, I been on the telephone calling; turns out there's not a lot of lucky fellas around. Arthur, ten thousand dollars.

ARTHUR
I—

MAX
I'm on the telephone calling up some of my former business associates; any one of them would jump at the opportunity. Unfortunately, they're all dead.
[*Outraged.*]
It's only twenty-two years; everybody died!

[*Sits at edge of pier, takes list of names from shopping bag.*]

Al Glickman, my meat supplier, *gone*—I'm speakin' to Al Glickman *Junior*. Kramer's Kitchen Supplies, I'm speakin' to Kramer Junior. Cantor and Sons, the contractor, I'm on the phone with "and Sons." How long I been gone? All of a sudden I'm living in New York Junior! And these Juniors, these winners, senior voices on the phone with junior guts, wouldn't advance you credit for a Hershey bar. Gotta know first, for *sure, every*thing—

[*Imitating their voices.*]

"Max *who*?" they say, "Hawaiian what? We'll see first how you do—after you open—maybe then . . ." Cold voices, people born for telephones . . .

[NANCY *approaches him at the pier, removing her hood. He looks at her, then at* ARTHUR, *suddenly laughing.*]

The joke is, what's payin' the phone bills for these darlings is a business they got from their fathers who wouldn't *trust* a voice on a telephone! Billy Gallino, Gallino Rolls and Buns—I'm talking yesterday to William . . . Gallino . . . Junior—a hundred receptionists answer the phone he shouldn't catch cancer from my voice—I ask him for credit, two months' goods, he gives me a cute maybe on the telephone.

[NANCY, *assuming that* MAX *doesn't recognize her, moves closer to him, becoming involved in what he is saying.*]

His father, I'll tell you frankly, was a thief. Overcharged me, sometimes delivered me stale merchandise; I'm sure he's not resting easy right now because he didn't steal the ground he's buried in. But Monday I'm on the phone with Junior and I'm sorry Billy isn't still alive to sell me yesterday's bread . . .

[*Suddenly standing, shouting; using the pier tie as support.*]

I'm sorry *none* of them are alive, those hondlers, those hustlers, those *faces*! Now I got the Maybe Babies! A dozen numbers I dialed and each place the *same fella* answered! You couldn't tell who, what, which one! Could be they all got together, hired a fella to make a record? O.K., their fathers had accents, but *they* got no sound at *all*! Billy Gallino, he read a bread order aloud, you could *tango* to it! We had a fight once on Canal Street. I hit him, he hit me—

[*Points to a mark over his eye.*]

Here's a scar from Gallino. We did business! Junior with his micey voice, he nibbles, he nibbles, he noshes on my soul. Billy, I knew what he was—Junior, he could be anything, a sea captain, a potato chip, a corn muffin, what?

[*A sudden burst of energy brings him to the end of the pier.*]

Ah-hah! But at the end of the conversation, these sweethearts'll do a "Goodbye" for you—oh *boy,* it's *beautiful*! "Hello," they don't do so good; and after "Hello," nervous and rotten . . . but "Goodbye," will *they* do a job for you on "Goodbye"!

[*He blows a goodbye kiss into the air.*]

"Goodbye . . . keep in touch . . . so long . . ." All of a sudden warm and personal and terrific . . .

[*Waving goodbye.*]

"Goodbye to ya . . . alla best to ya . . . we'll have lunch

. . . see ya around . . ." All of a sudden it's happiness, it's sweetness, it's their best number, it's the goodbye people and they're feelin' terrific; they got through a whole phone call without promising anything, without owing, they lived another day without getting into trouble . . .

[*He takes off his hat and waves it toward the ocean.*]

"Goodbye . . . goodbye . . . we're rootin' for ya . . . goodbye . . ."

[*He puts his hat back on; turns to them.*]

I'll tell ya the truth, buddy . . . the old days wasn't so terrific, but God help me from the new ones.

[*He picks up his shopping bag as if to leave; suddenly turns to* ARTHUR.]

Arthur, ten thousand dollars, I could open the store in two weeks; whaddya say?

ARTHUR

Ten thousand dollars, Jesus, I—

MAX

Eight then; seven . . .

ARTHUR

So suddenly, I—

MAX

Five. O.K., *five.* A full partnership for five . . .

ARTHUR

You see, it's—

MAX

Three! My final offer is three!

ARTHUR

Mr. Silverman, I'm—

MAX

Forget it! You lost it! It's finished!

ARTHUR

A sum like that, you can't expect a perfect stranger—

MAX

How perfect should a stranger be? Please, Mr. Sunrise, forget it.
[*Squeezing* ARTHUR's *face gently, as though he were an infant.*]
Arthur, darling, relax . . . sleep, my child.
[*Hoists the shopping bag up under his arm, turns to leave.*]
You just missed an opportunity, pure gold.
[*Walking briskly to the stairs.*]
I just figured you were in a generous mood. I mean, since you gave my daughter your coat, I figured maybe you'd give *me* a little something too . . .
[*He starts quickly up the steps.*]

NANCY
[*Startled, whispering.*]
  Pop . . .

MAX
[*He continues up the steps, singing.*]
  DO DE SWEET MAGNOLIAS BLOSSOM
  AT EVER'BODY'S DOOR?
  AND DO DE FOLKS KEEP EATIN' POSSUM,
  TILL DEY CAIN'T EAT NO MO' . . . ?
[*He turns left on the boardwalk, about to exit, still singing . . .*]

NANCY
[*Shouting up at him.*]
  No guilt, Silverman! Forget it! I'm booked ahead solid!
  I'm not free to feel guilty about you till the first Saturday
  in August! So forget it!
[*He continues walking, ignoring her, about to leave. She turns
angrily, wheeling her bike under the boardwalk, about to leave.*]

ARTHUR
  Hey, wait . . . Nancy . . . Mr. Silverman . . .

MAX
  Nancy? Nancy?
[*He turns.*]
  Who's Nancy? Where's Nancy?

NANCY
[*Stepping out from under the boardwalk.*]
   Me. I changed my name to Nancy Scott.

MAX
   Terrific.

NANCY
   I kept the *S*.

MAX
   Wonderful.
[*He turns to leave.*]

NANCY
   Pop, wait . . . hey, Silverman . . .

MAX
   Silverman? Who's Silverman? There's no Silverman
here . . .
[*He turns to them.*]
   Allow me to introduce myself. Ricky Rogers. How do you
do?

NANCY
   O.K., Pop—

MAX
   I kept the *R*.

NANCY

O.K., Pop, get it all out; now tell me about my new nose. Go ahead—

MAX

What nose? I don't see a nose. Arthur, do you see a nose?

NANCY

It's not that small—

MAX

First try and hold up a pair of glasses with it, then we'll talk. Whatsa matter, they couldn't leave you with something? They took away a nose and left a message. Listen, Mary-Lou, I'll tell ya—

NANCY

It's *Nancy*—

MAX

Excuse me, it's hard to remember a name when you don't know the face.

NANCY

It happens to be a damn good job, Pop—

MAX

Sure it's a good job. For a pixie. For a person it's ridiculous.

ARTHUR
Actually, Mr. Silverman, a pixie's nose is quite—

MAX
Ah, the daredevil speaks! What's with you and Captain Courageous here; funny business on the beach?

NANCY
Pop, *Jesus*—

MAX
Right, that's the name; Jesus. Used to be Max, but I changed it to reach a bigger crowd.
[*Standing firm at the top of the stairs, he stares off at the horizon now, refusing to look down at her.*]
Some people are in the hospital for three months. Some people don't come to visit them. That's some people.

NANCY
Pop, I didn't even *know*, I—

MAX
Some people didn't even know. So out of touch, certain parties are. That's certain parties.

NANCY
O.K., Pop . . . you got all the aces . . .
[*Sits, defeated, on bottom step.*]
The hospital, I didn't know; I never think of you as being

sick. Pop, I listen to you talking about the guys you spoke to on the phone . . . and I realize how much I need you to be alive.

[*He remains looking the other way; makes an elaborate business of shifting his shopping bag from one hand to the other.*]

Silverman; you gonna keep standing up there like that?

MAX

You; you gonna keep sittin' down there like that?

NANCY

[*Taking a deep breath.*]

The air; you can taste it out here . . . damp and salty and full of Silverman pride.

MAX

Silverman? I see only one Silverman! One Silverman and one runaway nose-fixer in a stranger's coat! The victim of a recent massive coronary stands here waiting for an explanation.

NANCY

[*She suddenly stands, shouting.*]

O.K., Silverman, I have seen your vengeful moods before! Your ears close, your accent gets thicker, and Zorro rides again! You don't *want* an explanation; you just want me to stand here and keep feeding you straight lines! Either you warm up a little and *talk* to me or I'm on my way . . .

MAX
Threats, ultimatums . . .

NANCY
Well, what's it gonna be, Silverman?

MAX
Deals, negotiations . . .
[*He remains silently looking the other way, straightening his hat.*
ARTHUR *looks tensely from one to the other.*]

NANCY
Well . . . I tried . . .
[*She turns sharply, wheeling her bike quickly off left under the boardwalk.*]

MAX
Sally-Ann . . .
[*She stops.*]
You see that stairway there?
[*Still not looking at her, he gestures toward the stairs.*]
It has got, by actual count, twenty-two steps. You show up on step number eleven, and maybe I'll meet you there shortly.
[*She looks up at him.*]
I heard a weather report on the radio this morning. Says cold air masses are coming down from Canada.
[*He turns, smiles, holds out his arms to her.*]
Quickly, quickly . . . before they get here . . .

[*She laughs, drops her bike, and races up the steps into his arms.*]
Devochka, devochka . . . welcome to the top of the stairs.

NANCY

"Devochka," doesn't that mean—

MAX

It means you fixed your nose but I love you anyway.
[*They sit on the top step; she holds his hands in hers.* ARTHUR, *unnoticed by them, has been moved almost to tears by their reconciliation; sits on dune, watching with pleasure and fascination.*]

NANCY

O.K. now, Pop, admit it; I don't look so bad.

MAX

Certainly you are a pretty person. But once you were a novelty item; now regular merchandise.

NANCY

Pop, I just wanted things to be new . . .

MAX

Must be a good attitude because I got the exact same attitude; that's why I'm opening the store again—

NANCY

Pop, the store—

MAX

I'll tell you what chance you got to talk me out of it. No chance.

NANCY

But you're not well—

MAX

Not well is twenty-two years workin' for somebody else, that's a disease you can die from—

NANCY

How ya gonna do it alone?

MAX

What's alone? Comes back with me, once a partner, still a gentleman and a genius, Marcus Soloway!

NANCY

You spoke to him . . .

MAX

Not for a couple years . . . but I'll fix the store like it was, he'll see it, he'll join right up! I know what's in that classy Soloway head! He owns still fifty percent of the property, it's valuable, it's beach-front. Like me, a hundred times Marcus coulda sold his share. But he keeps it twenty-two years. Why? Because, like me, he's got the same idea! Because, like me, he waits for our turn to come again . . .

[*He stands.*]

You're thinking I'm crazy, why open? Who'll come in the winter? People come; for the best, people come . . . for ecstasy they show up . . .

NANCY

But, to fix up the store, where will you get the money from?

MAX

Where will I get the money from? I'll . . . I'll *tell* you where I'll get the money from!

ARTHUR

From me . . .

MAX

From *him*! I'll get the money from him!

[*Turns, looks down at* ARTHUR.]

From him . . . ?

[NANCY, *also surprised, looks down at* ARTHUR. ARTHUR *stands on top of the dune, a little surprised himself.*]

ARTHUR

[*Quietly*]

I've been thinking about it . . . and I've decided to invest in this . . .

[*Gestures to store.*]

. . . this project here, yes . . .

[*Slides to bottom of dune.*]
   Property, yes . . . property at the beach . . .
[*He touches the store; the little building shudders with age.*]

MAX
[*Coming quickly down the stairs to him.*]
   Congratulations, Mr. Sunrise, you just made a first-class
   investment—

NANCY
   Arthur, why the hell're you—

MAX
   Close-'em-up-the-mouth, Mary Jane—

ARTHUR
   Actually, I *would* like to tell you why. You see, Mr. Silverman, I've—

MAX
   For ten thousand dollars you can call me Max—

ARTHUR
   O.K., Max, I—

MAX
   I said for ten thousand dollars. Until I get the check keep
   calling me Mr. Silverman—

NANCY

Let him finish what he's *saying,* I wanna know why the hell he's—

MAX

[*Sharply, aside*]

No-sir, this kinda fella you let him open his mouth he'll talk himself right out of it—

ARTHUR

[*A slight tremor in his voice.*]

You see, a time comes when one must—

NANCY

[*Coming urgently down the steps.*]

Arthur, it's *February,* he's not *well;* what do ya think you're *doing?* Being *nice?* Doing us a *favor?*

MAX

[*Offended; gesturing grandly.*]

What nice? What favor? He's waltzing into a gold mine!

ARTHUR

[*With genuine admiration*]

Jesus, Mr. Silverman, how do ya do it? You just *believe* that everything's gonna work out for ya, you just—

MAX

Crap! I don't believe in *noth*ing or *no*body!

[*Pokes* ARTHUR's *chest.*]

Including *you* till I get my check.

[*As he busily takes shopping bag from stairs, begins removing items from it: blueprints, deeds, sandwiches, pens, contracts, a thermos bottle, zoning maps, etc.*]

I believe in *me, Max;* and why's that? Because I'm terrific? No-sir. Because I'm what's left. Hello and goodbye; I look around, what's left is me. Willy and nilly, what's left is me. I believe in Max Silverman, and when the weather is nice I believe in God; a couple days in the spring and that's *that* . . .

[*Takes two new pamphlets from bag.*]

Meanwhile, darling; if God don't work out . . . there's contracts. Sign this and a check and then we'll *all* believe . . .

[*Smooths out a plateau of sand on the side of the dune, lays out the contracts on it, hands* ARTHUR *a pen.*]

The signed contracts you'll take to Michael David Silverman, a lawyer and a son . . .

NANCY

[*Approaching them.*]

Pop, wait . . .

MAX

His address is on the top there . . .

NANCY

Both of you, please . . . look; the Alamo with pineapples, look . . .

MAX

[*Ignores her, reading contract softly to* ARTHUR.]

"Joint Venture Agreement . . ." Beautiful, all poetry . . . "The party of the second part, hereinafter referred to as Joint Venturer . . ." That's you, darling; yesterday a sleeper, today a party and a venturer! Says here also, "Right of Survivorship"; means one of us dies, the other one gets the entire kaboodle. Arthur, if you don't drop dead, you got a terrific deal here . . .

NANCY

Snow, it's gonna snow next week . . .

MAX

Now the best part . . . paragraph 7 . . .

[*Softly: a hymn.*]

"The party of the first part does hereby grant joint ownership of the property to the party of the second part . . . and to all his heirs and successors forever . . ." Ah, such words . . . a contract like this you don't need a lawyer, you get a mixed chorus to sing it to you . . .

[ARTHUR'*s pen is poised over the contract.*]

Your name is Arthur Korman . . .

[ARTHUR *suddenly signs.* MAX *snaps it away and flashes a second copy under* ARTHUR'*s pen.* ARTHUR *signs the second one.*]

NANCY
[*Sits helplessly on the stairs.*]
　　Oh, God . . .

ARTHUR
[*Quietly*]
　　A short name . . . what a short name I've got . . .

MAX
[*Softly*]
　　Arthur . . . you know what this means . . . ?
They have been seated at the dune; MAX *rises now and extends his hand to* ARTHUR.]
　　It means shake the hand . . .
[ARTHUR *rises unsteadily, takes* MAX's *hand.*]
　　Shake the hand and you own a piece of the world for-
　　ever . . .
[*There is a gust of whistling wind; it rattles the papers on the beach. The men stand with their hands joined, the lights dim;* NANCY *shivers, looking up at the winter sky as* . . .

　　　　　　　　　　　　　THE CURTAIN FALLS]

ACT TWO

Before the curtain goes up we hear a scratchy old record of Al Jolson singing a Hawaiian love song . . .

JOLSON'S VOICE
  DOWN HAWAII WAY
  WHERE I CHANCED TO STRAY
  ON AN EVENIN' I HEARD
  A HULA MAIDEN SAY . . .
[ARTHUR'S *voice joins in softly.*]

ARTHUR and JOLSON'S VOICE
  YAAKA HULA HICKEY DULA
  YAAKA HULA HICKEY DU . . .
[*As the curtain rises*]
  DOWN HAWAII WAY
  BY THE MOONLIT BAY
  WHERE I LINGERED AWHILE, SHE
  STOLE M'HEART AWAY . . .

[*It is early evening; the boardwalk lamps are lit, there is moonlight and a gentle glow on the sand. Everything else is as it was, with one extraordinary exception—to the left of the store is a rather well sculpted seven-foot palm tree; it is arched gracefully over the store and over* ARTHUR, *who sits beneath it holding his banjo and singing quietly in the moonlight.*

To his right, tacked onto one of the boardwalk pillars, is his designer's "rendering" of the projected Hawaiian Ecstasies, in which the store is seen in all its imagined glory—many palm trees, tables and chairs spread along the beach; the store itself is pictured as a multicolored grass hut, the roof features a glowing Hawaiian volcano, and towering above that is a neon frankfurter. The actual steps toward realizing the rendering are small at this point, but promising; there is the tree that ARTHUR *is building, and just downstage of it a wicker table and two small wicker chairs; an open carton marked "Colby's Outdoor Products— Everything under the Sun" stands nearby. Several of the boards have been removed from the front of the store, partially revealing the old counter; an ancient portable Victrola rests on the counter, from which the music continues . . .*]

YAAKA HULA HICKEY DULA

YAAKA HULA HICKEY DU . . .

[*He hits two chords on his banjo; chuckles with satisfaction, goes on with the song.*]

OH, I DON'T CARE IF YOU'VE LOVED THE LADIES

FAR AND NEAR . . .

[*Rises, continues work on the tree, molding swirls of bark around the trunk.*]

YOU'LL FORGET ABOUT 'EM ALL IF

YOU COULD HEAR

YAAKA HULA HICKEY DULA

YAAKA HULA HICKEY DU . . .

[*There is a gust of wind; the tree begins to sway. He hugs the tree to steady it. The phone rings. He continues to hold on to the tree, singing softly.*]

YAAKA HULA HICKEY DULA

YAAKA HICKEY DU . . .

[*The phone continues to ring, piercing the gentle moonlit setting and the soft music.* ARTHUR *finally lets go of the tree, turns the music off, walks decisively to the phone booth, humming a bit more of the song . . . shifting unconsciously to "Jingle Bells" as he reaches the booth. Grabs phone; speaks briskly.*]

ARTHUR

Arthur Korman here! Right, Bill; how the hell are ya, fella? Well now, where were we? We haven't talked so we couldn't be anywhere, right? O.K., here's the situation, Bill; here's how it shapes up . . . That's because it *is* rolling surf, Bill . . . Right, but this is a very nice time of year also. Picturesque . . . Glad that amuses you, Bill; but the fact is . . .

[*Looks at horizon for inspiration. There is only the moon.*]

The fact is I'm involved in a very interesting project here at the beach, Bill . . . a design project of my own, and I might well continue to . . . A restaurant, I guess you might call it a sort of an outdoor restaurant, a sort of an

outdoor-restaurant-beach-design project is what I'm involved in here, Bill . . . I wish you wouldn't do that . . .
Bill, I'd really rather you didn't laugh at this . . .

[*Sits in booth; quietly*]

Don't laugh, please . . .

[NANCY *enters on boardwalk, at right, wearing his Mackinaw and
carrying a portable electric heater. She stands at the top of the
stairs, unnoticed by him, listening.*]

Quitting? Quitting? Who said that? Oh; well, she's an
associate of mine here at the project, poor kid's been under
a lot of pressure; fact is, we're all under a lot of pressure
here at the project right now, so I'd appreciate your calling
me back in ten minutes because there's something important I have to discuss with you, Bill, a whole area of dis-
cussion. Beautiful; finish your dinner and call me back.
That'll be beautiful. I really appreciate your cooperation on
this, Bill. Later, man. Beautiful. 'Bye.

[*Hangs up quickly; slumps in booth, exhausted. Sees* NANCY *at
the top of the stairs.*]

Oh . . .

[*Leaves booth.*]

Good evening. I'm glad to see you . . .

[*She remains at the top of the stairs, looking the other way.*]

I was just discussing the quitting area with Bill.

[*Silence. He gestures about.*]

Well, Max and I . . . we've begun. How do you like the
tree? The tree here . . .

[*Silence. No reply.*]

It's just Celanese strips over aluminum armature, but I think you still get this graceful-tree feeling . . .
[*Touching the tree.*]
Used all of my old tools . . .
[*He bounds over to the wicker table.*]
Hey, first table sample in from Colby's—
[*Takes umbrella from under table; fits it into center of table, opens it. It is in the shape of a small palm tree.*]
Sort of a follow-through here on the graceful-tree feeling, see, it's—

NANCY
[*Quietly, calmly*]
You've gone mad.

ARTHUR
I'm sorry you feel that way . . .

NANCY
You have set sail on the banana boat.

ARTHUR
I really wish you'd consider the—

NANCY
[*Shouting.*]
Crazy! The word is "crazy"! A man who can't play the banjo and an old man who can't lift one are gonna sell frankfurters on the beach in the dead of winter!

ARTHUR

Well, it's a unique enterprise, that's true, but—

NANCY

Graceful-tree feeling! Oh, my God—

ARTHUR

And you're wrong; I can play the banjo—
[*Picks it up, strums two chords.*]

NANCY

Oh, Jesus—

ARTHUR

Well, I'm still learning—

NANCY

Dead of winter! Dead as in dying! As in dying old man!
I saw you with my own eyes, I saw you give him a check
for ten thousand dollars! That's not a *business* investment,
that's *funeral* expenses, that's—

ARTHUR

How much did you give him?

NANCY

Two thousand.
[*Sits on top step; quietly*]
How could I do that? I don't understand; I went with him

to deposit your check, to talk him out of it, and the next thing I knew . . . How could I do that? I asked Dr. Berman about it this afternoon . . .

ARTHUR

What did he say?

NANCY

He said the best he could do was three hundred.

MAX'S VOICE

[*Approaching, at left, singing.*]

MOONLIGHT BECOMES YOU,

IT GOES WITH YOUR FACE,

YOU CERTAINLY KNOW HOW

TO FIX YOURSELF UP TERRIFIC . . .

NANCY

I'm trapped, mister. I can't stop him, and I can't leave him either, I . . .

MAX

[*Enters on boardwalk, carrying two large toolboxes; singing.*]

MOONLIGHT BECOMES YOU,

I'LL TELL YOU RIGHT NOW . . .

[*Sees* ARTHUR'*s tree; stops, deeply impressed. He takes a step down the stairs, looks at the tree in the moonlight; whispering.*]

Oh . . . oh, boy . . .

NANCY

Pop, you shouldn't be carrying all those—

MAX

[*Quietly, to* ARTHUR]

What can be said? O.K., a partner . . . a friend even, I figured. But an artist, a great artist, I was not prepared . . .

[*Coming quickly down the stairs.*]

The Last Supper? Forget it! A comic strip! The *Mona Lisa* is a bimbo! Move over, God, we got another fella here makes trees!

[*Squeezes* ARTHUR'*s face.*]

Your check goes today into Irving Trust, smooth . . . smooth like an egg into a cake, and all day my ear is filled with "yes" . . . "yes" from Auerbach Refrigeration, "yes" from Holiday Juice Machine, "yes" from—

NANCY

[*Trying to take one of the toolboxes.*]

Here, let me—

MAX

Same nose from this morning? Good. I'm getting used to it.

[*Goes to counter with toolboxes, sets them down.*]

Partner, up the street by Shatzkin's Famous Knishes, is James Carlos Velásquez—a Spanish gentleman, a cabdriver, and a visionary. A small percentage, deferred, he does our deliveries here—

[*Points to street.*]

Go; look for a young fella, sixty-eight, with a Dodge, '73 —inside is a new sign for the store, unpainted. Bring it and paint it!

ARTHUR
[*Indicates rendering.*]

Max, I'd like to discuss—

MAX

At my earliest possible convenience—
[*Points, under boardwalk.*]

Shirley, two blocks down Stillwell, a Pittsburgh Paint Outlet. They're open ten more minutes; establish credit and bring me a rainbow.
[*He looks at them both.*]

What I got here? Sand castles?
[*Claps his hands.*]

Move . . . Move . . . Time. Time. A couple weeks we open here!

[NANCY *exits reluctantly under the boardwalk.* ARTHUR *hesitates on the stairs.*]

O.K., I'll look at the picture . . .
[*Goes to rendering; studies it for several moments. Turns solemnly to* ARTHUR.]

I'll tell ya what you're talkin' here, mister . . . you're talkin' ecstasy.

ARTHUR
I think we need some really big palm trees, Max—

MAX
No others would be acceptable!

ARTHUR
The volcano on the roof, I—

MAX
Guaranteed, a volcano!

ARTHUR
[*Going quickly up the stairs.*]
Grass huts!

MAX
I love it!

ARTHUR
[*Exits to right, on boardwalk.*]
Tribal masks!

MAX
A must! Whatever they are!
[*Alone now; looks at rendering.*]
A little dull; but he'll learn.
[*Takes crowbar from toolbox, begins prying loose the first of the boards covering the front of the store; singing.*]

MOONLIGHT BECOMES YOU,

I'M NOT KIDDING AROUND . . .

[*The phone rings. He grabs it, instinctively distrusting the instrument.*]

What is it, who is it? I'm busy here! . . . The what? The beach project? Correct, yessir, this is the beach project. I'm the chairman. State your business . . . He's not here. Later, call later. Sunrise is a good time . . .

[*During these last few moments, a* MAN *has entered on the boardwalk at left. He stands in the spill of light from one of the boardwalk lamps, a silhouette carrying a briefcase, looking down at the proceedings . . . During the next few lines he comes down the stairs, looking solemnly about at the palm tree, the wicker table, the rendering. A rather neatly dressed man in his late thirties, his air of efficiency and organization is immediately at odds with the beach and the open sky. His attitude and his clothes belong to closed rooms. He will be constantly brushing sand off his shoes and his well-pressed overcoat.*

He very carefully places his briefcase out of sight under the wicker table, then watches MAX *finish his conversation.*]

Who may I say rang? Who? Bill? Bill, from "Goodbye, Bill"? Listen, he's got a girl friend now, leave him alone. Palm trees, girls, a healthy life by the sea; it's not too late for *you,* either.

[*Sits in booth.*]

Tell me something, what line are you in? . . . Jingle Bells? Sounds risky. Seasonal and risky. Listen to me, you want to get involved with something sturdy, with a foundation? Do yourself a favor, Billy; come down, give a glance

here; Tenth Street and the boardwalk. Look for the volcano!
[*Hangs up.*]

MAN

My God . . . what's this?

MAX
[*Turns to him.*]
What's this? What does it look like? It's paradise. Who
are you?
[*Leaves booth, studying the* MAN's *face.*]
Wait . . . I know you from some place . . .

MAN
[*Sits on wicker chair.*]
Take a second, Max. It'll come back to you.

MAX

Atlantic City, nineteen fifty-eight . . .

MAN
No.

MAX

Sure; business. I know you from business . . .

MAN
No.

MAX
Wait, wait, a *relative* . . .

MAN
Right.

MAX
A cousin, a nephew, a . . .

MAN
A son. I'm your son.

MAX
Which one?

MAN
Michael.

MAX
[*Snaps his fingers.*]
Of course, my son Michael. Must be him. Looks just like him.
[*Shakes his hand, cordially*]
How-do-you-do-sir.

MICHAEL
Max, there are some urgent legal matters—

MAX

Sure, now I remember. My lawyer, the son. See, at first I couldn't recognize; because a son, you make a simple cash request—

[*Points to store.*]

—an investment in paradise, he doesn't tell you to go to hell—

MICHAEL

Max, I refuse to finance your suicide—

MAX

Even a lawyer, what's the good? I give you something to handle, a simple divorce—

MICHAEL

A simple divorce? My mother and father; a simple divorce? Max, I told you, this insane divorce, you have no right to ask me. You'll have to get a stranger—

MAX

With a son like you, who needs a stranger?

MICHAEL

Max, get another lawyer—

MAX

What do I pay you?

MICHAEL

Nothing.

MAX

Then I'll wait till I get a better buy.

MICHAEL

Max, there is another, quite imperative matter which I have attempted, unsuccessfully, to bring to your attention—

MAX

Who stops you?

MICHAEL

Max, I came to the house last week and you threw me out. I came in, you hollered, "Yich! Briefcase-carrier!" And shoved me out the door.

MAX

You shouldn't bring a briefcase to dinner. It's not nice.

MICHAEL

And now the matter has increased in urgency.
[*Taking* ARTHUR's *contract from his overcoat pocket.*]
Max, some fellow named Korman left this on my secretary's desk this morning—

MAX
[*Glancing about.*]
Hey, where you got it?

MICHAEL

What?

MAX

The briefcase, where you got it?

MICHAEL

Out of sight, don't be concerned . . .

MAX

[*Pleasantly*]

Where you got it? Let me see . . .

MICHAEL

[*Lifts it out from under table.*]

Here, I've—

MAX

[*Shouting.*]

Yich! Briefcase-carrier! Old man! Go away!

MICHAEL

[*Quickly putting case back under table.*]

It's gone, Max, it's gone—

MAX

In a briefcase comes always bad news. Now you got worse anyway; that suit. A suit for old people. A suit to be buried in. Or to bury somebody . . .

[*Sits opposite him; quietly*]

Tell me: you came here to bury somebody . . . ?

MICHAEL

Max, if we're finished with my briefcase and my suit, there is an urgent legal matter—

MAX

The tone, the voice, I don't like it—

MICHAEL

What *do* you like about me?

MAX

Since eighteen: nothing. You went into the boredom business, became a pioneer in the field—

[*Bangs on the table.*]

The *looks* of you. Old. Old. Go eat a hamburger, get a *stain* on yourself, wear the wrong *tie, something*. What happened to sloppy kids?

MICHAEL

I'm not a kid, Max—

MAX

Sure, a kid—

MICHAEL

Max, I have a profession, a wife, two sons—

MAX

Two? How nice for you; I don't have *any*.
[*Rising.*]
Now you'll excuse me, I open here soon, there are touches
to finish—

MICHAEL

Max, wait, we've got to talk—
[*Quietly*]
Max, have you spoken to Soloway . . . ?

MAX

What's to speak? When I finish the store, I'll call him,
he'll join right up—

MICHAEL

Max, to begin with . . . believe me, I never expected you
to be able to get *any*body to invest in—

MAX

What's to tell me?

MICHAEL

It seemed reasonable to assume—

MAX
[*Coming toward the table.*]
What's to tell me, Michael?

MICHAEL

Please remember, you were in the hospital, you were not expected to survive—

MAX

What, the cemetery is suing me for breach of promise?

MICHAEL

The store had just been sitting here for years . . . of no use to anybody . . . there was Mother to consider, an income to consider . . .

MAX

What, what . . . ?

MICHAEL

Max . . .

MAX

What, what, what—?

MICHAEL

Max, the property was sold. A month ago, when you were in the hospital . . .

[MAX *is quite calm; he sits opposite* MICHAEL *at the table.*]

Max, please understand, it's just this week you've talked about reopening . . . after all these years . . .

MAX
[*Quietly, calmly*]
Sold. To who, sold?

MICHAEL
The Mister Hot Dog stores. It's a chain of—

MAX
I have seen them.

MICHAEL
They're always interested in beach-front locations, they—

MAX
You have received a check? You have cash in the hand?

MICHAEL
Not yet.

MAX
And Marcus. He agreed? He is selling his share?

MICHAEL
Yes.

MAX
[*Lights his cigar; leans back calmly in his chair.*]
Uh-huh.

MICHAEL

Max, I hope you understand; I acted in what appeared to be the best interests of . . .

MAX

Certainly.

MICHAEL

You see, we all thought . . .

MAX

Certainly; you all thought I was passing away . . .
[*Without rising,* MAX *suddenly grabs the lapels of* MICHAEL's *overcoat and pulls him across the table.*]
Well, I passed back in again, Sonny Boy . . .
[*Pulling him closer.*]
Tell Mister Hot Dog the deal is off! Tell him Max had a change of heart; it's still beating!

MICHAEL

Max, listen to me—

MAX

There's no conversation—
[*Lets go of him.*]
Refuse the money—

MICHAEL

Max, you don't have to *take* the money, they're quite will-

ing to offer you a percentage of the profits instead. They'll
put one of their stores here this summer, you'll share in
all the—

MAX

Here? In paradise?
[*Rises from table.*]
They'll put up a Mister Hot Dog in paradise?

MICHAEL

Please, Max . . . don't you see, you won't have to knock
yourself out. And you'll still be in *business,* you'll be a
partner, you'll drop around from time to time . . . like
your brother Harry and the hardware store . . .

MAX

I don't want to do business like my brother Harry, and I
don't wanna shimmy like my sister Kate neither! Partners
with *them?* Garbage merchants! The answer is out of the
question.
[*Goes to front of store, continues prying board loose with crowbar.*]

MICHAEL
[*Follows* MAX *to store.*]
Max, I *told* you, they're getting Soloway's share, they'll *be*
your partners whether you sell or not. They're going to
want one of their chain stores here by June 15, for the summer season—

MAX
[*Turns to him with crowbar.*]
My regrets to Mister Hot Dog, also *Mrs.* Hot Dog—

MICHAEL
Max, unless you can prove you're running a profitable business here by June, they've got the legal right to put up one
of their own—

MAX
Profits; there'll *be* profits!

MICHAEL
How, Max? From what?

MAX
From business! From customers! It's almost springtime!

MICHAEL
Max, they'll take you to *court,* it's—

MAX
Gorgeous! Court is gorgeous!
[*Delighted, he grips* MICHAEL'*s arm.*]
Everybody sues everybody! Meanwhile the store is open,
meanwhile profits! They'll take you to court, you'll *keep*
them there. Delays and stalling, legal monkey business.
You'll do it, Michael; you and the magic briefcase. Get me
time, get me the summer, and I'll show you profits . . .

MICHAEL

Max, there won't *be* any profits . . . not here . . . there never were . . .

MAX

Take a sniff that breeze, there's gold in the air . . .

MICHAEL

Max, no . . . we can't . . .

MAX

Why *no*? Why *can't*?
[*Holding* MICHAEL's *arm, shaking him.*]
Do it, Michael! Do this thing! Do a silly thing! Get a wrinkle in your suit! Give me a sign I'll know you're alive . . .

MICHAEL

[*Quietly*]
Max, please . . . this place won't last a month. And if *it* does, *you* won't. It's foolish, it's impossible . . . it'll kill you, Max.

MAX

[*Lets go of his arm.*]
When you were a baby, you were smart. At three months you knew to wave bye-bye . . .
[*Walks away from him to counter.*]
It's still the thing you do best.

MICHAEL

Max, I'm trying to—

MAX

Soloway, he made a contract?

MICHAEL

Not yet, they're negotiating; but by the end of the week
they—

MAX

[*Delighted*]
He's negotiating. Perfect.
[*Returns to work, prying board with crowbar.*]
Now you may leave the premises.

MICHAEL

Max, I'm—

MAX

[*Shouts.*]
Kindly leave the premises!

MICHAEL

It never varies, Max. Whenever I see you, you say the same
three things to me: "Hello," "Who are you?" and "Leave
the premises."
[*Going to table.*]
Actually, Max, since eighteen I haven't been too crazy
about *you* either.

[*Picks up briefcase.*]

You keep telling me I'm ashamed of your accent. I never was. Only mystified. I just can't figure out why it's thicker now than it was twenty years ago . . .

[*Turns to him.*]

The anger too. Thicker and thicker. Today I'm trying to talk you into staying alive, and you're angry. You were angry last year, and year before that, and three years ago you came to my house for dinner . . . and asked me to leave the premises. My own home, Max; y'know, the one with the two sons . . . ?

[MAX *ignores him, busily prying board with crowbar.*

ARTHUR *enters at right on boardwalk carrying large wooden sign. Stops, listens, unnoticed by them.*]

Tell me, Max; what is it? Solve the mystery. What makes you perpetually angry with me?

[MAX *continues his work.* MICHAEL *raises his voice, almost shouting.*]

Come *on,* Max! I'm *asking you*—my client, the father! *What the hell is*—

[*Checks himself; regains control; speaks quietly again.*]

Well, it's certainly not going to accomplish anything for *both* of us to get angry—

[*Picks up his briefcase, about to exit.*]

No point in . . .

MAX

[*Quietly*]

Wait a minute . . .

[*Points with crowbar.*]

What you were just doing here . . . *that* was angry? What kinda angry is that, I don't know till you tell me? Here, I'll show you angry . . .

[MAX *suddenly smashes one of the boards with his crowbar, shouting.*]

This is angry!

[*Quietly, smiling.*]

You see that? There's no mix-up.

[*Coming toward* MICHAEL.]

There's the mystery, *that's* why I'm angry—because I never know when *you* are. I look in your face: what's up? If that's angry, it's not enough. I look in your face, I don't see anybody. I look for Max, I don't see him either . . . that's why I got a store. The accent? Was a time, there were neighborhoods in this city I could cash checks with it. Whatta *you* got tells you you're not somebody else? An American Express card? The store is foolish, the store is silly, but the store is mine. Whatta you got belongs to *you*? A briefcase fulla bad news and an old man's suit. Go away from me, you're breaking my eyes. Wave bye-bye, sonny, I'll see you in a million years . . .

[MAX *takes ledger pad from overcoat pocket, sits at table with his back to* MICHAEL, *checking figures with a pencil stub.* MICHAEL *turns to leave, stops.*]

MICHAEL

Max, you're going to open the store . . .

MAX

Of course.

MICHAEL

Then I'm quite certain I won't see you alive again.

MAX

Get a Polaroid. Take a picture.

MICHAEL

I don't understand . . .
[*Shouts.*]
God damn you, Max . . . why do you want to die here
with a bunch of palm trees!
[*Covers his eyes with his hand.*]
Damn you, damn you, old man; I'm crying . . .

MAX

You feel so bad, help me to open the store.

MICHAEL

I can't help you to kill yourself, Max.

MAX

[*Turns to him.*]
Yessir, you're crying . . . but not enough!
[*Turns abruptly back to the ledger, immediately absorbed.*]
"Six counter grills, double weight, two hundred eighty,
installed . . ."

[MICHAEL *steps forward violently, about to smash his fist into the table—checks himself, composes himself; turns to leave.*]

"Malt mixers, eight-speed, gallon size, with filter . . ."

[MICHAEL *remembers that he has left his briefcase, picks it up, exits quickly under the boardwalk at right, brushing the sand off his briefcase.*]

"Quart-size, twenty-two eighty, repairs up to one year . . ."

NANCY'S VOICE
    Pop . . .

[*She steps solemnly out of the shadows under the boardwalk, at left, carrying carton of paints. She has apparently been standing there for some time.*]

NANCY
    Pop, I was . . .

MAX
[*Rises, goes toward her.*]
    Ah, the colors . . .

NANCY
    Pop, I heard . . .

MAX
    All?

NANCY
    Enough.

MAX

Good. Then you know there's nothing to worry—
[*Smiling, takes carton of paints from her.*]

NANCY

[*To* ARTHUR, *who is carrying the sign down the stairs.*]
Arthur, Soloway's selling his share to the Mister Hot Dog
chain . . .

ARTHUR

Oh, God—

MAX

I don't need "Oh, God" from you, I can get "Oh, God"
from her.
[*Happily opening the carton of paints.*]
Nothing to worry, plenty time. He's not *selling,* he's
negotiating. Like people *breathe,* Soloway negotiates. In a
subway he negotiates the carfare—

ARTHUR

Max, if he sells—

MAX

Darling, darling, if he knew we were opening he wouldn't
enter*tain* such an offer, wouldn't even give it a cookie.
Be advised, sir; we are talking here of Marcus Soloway
. . . a man built temples in the sand, sea lions, pillars
toward the sky . . .

[*His arm around* ARTHUR.]

Arthur, wait'll he sees your volcano . . . your trees . . .

[*Points to rendering.*]

How much can we do in three days?

ARTHUR

Well . . . some, I—

MAX

"Some" is exactly enough!

[*Shakes* ARTHUR'*s hand.*]

It's settled; we open in three days!

NANCY

Oh, God . . .

MAX

See how good she does it?

[*His hand on* ARTHUR'*s shoulder.*]

Arthur, all we gotta do is show Marcus we're in business, show him we're alive . . . I promise you, he'll join right up.

[*Quietly*]

Partner . . . do you trust me on this?

ARTHUR

Well, yes, I—

MAX

Then what're ya hangin' around for!

[*Points to sign.*]

The letters are there, fill me in the colors! Sunrise, Arthur; fix me colors like the sunrise!

[*Hands crowbar to* NANCY.]

Quickly, the boards come off the store; tomorrow equipment arrives! Installations!

[*Walking briskly to stairs.*]

Some words in English are beautiful. "Installations" is beautiful. "Deliveries" is beautiful.

[*Going up the stairs.*]

"Goods," "equipment," "counter," "register" . . .

NANCY

Where are you going?

MAX

The première has been advanced, I must go now to Margolis on the corner—formerly tailor of Florenz Ziegfeld, "Flo" to him—makes me an outfit for the opening, stripes; stripes to dazzle the eye . . .

NANCY

Pop, wait . . .

MAX

"Wait" is not a beautiful word . . .

[*As he exits*]

"Wholesale" is a beautiful word. "Contract" is another beauty . . .

[*Disappearing to the left down the boardwalk.*]

"Percentage," "price," "bargain," "customer," "sale" . . .

NANCY

[*Quietly*]

I can't do it.

[*To* ARTHUR]

Nope. Sorry. Can't.

[*Shakes her head.*]

Uh-uh.

[*He approaches her.*]

I can't. I can't watch this. I thought I could; but I can't . . .

[*She hands him the crowbar.*]

I have to leave now.

[*Points to heater she brought earlier.*]

That's portable; make sure he uses it to keep warm . . .

[*Going left, under boardwalk.*]

Promise me . . .

ARTHUR

Nancy, I think we should try to—

NANCY

Arthur, you're a nice man, a gentle man; but you're quite crazy. You're both crazy and I have to leave now.

ARTHUR
[*Gestures to store.*]
The three of us together, maybe we could—

NANCY
It's a wonderful group. I don't know who I am, he's dying, and you can't quit your job.
[*She starts to exit left under the boardwalk.*

ARTHUR *suddenly hauls back and smashes the crowbar against the stairway railing; the sound rings in the air—she turns, startled.*]

ARTHUR
All right, goddamn it, that's it!
[*He flings open the phone booth door.*]
Gotta be done, the time has come!
[*Deposits coin, dialing fiercely.*]
No more foolin' around here . . . damn it . . .
[*The phone in the second booth starts to ring.*]

NANCY
Arthur, he's calling you back! Arthur, the other phone!
[*He ignores her, bent on his mission.*]
Arthur!
[*She races to the second booth, grabs the phone.*]
Bill, listen; Arthur's calling you on the other—

ARTHUR
Hello.

NANCY
Hello. Listen, he's—

ARTHUR
Hello, Nancy?

NANCY
Who is this?

ARTHUR
It's me, Arthur.

NANCY
Arthur . . .

ARTHUR
Look, I tell ya why I called . . .

NANCY
Arthur, I'm hanging up now . . .
[*Leans around corner of booth; speaking directly to his back.*]
Arthur, I'm hanging up now, O.K.?

ARTHUR
Nancy, don't go—
[*He grips the phone tensely.*]
Nancy, I'm twenty minutes late for *every*thing; conversations, trains, sunrises, people . . . Being alive; I'm twenty

years late on that one. So don't go, Nancy, not now . . .
not now, I just got here.
[*Touched by what he has said, she delicately, soundlessly hangs
up her phone, leaves her booth, stands behind him. Unaware, he
continues on the phone.*]
Hello? Hello, Nancy . . . ?

NANCY
[*Quietly*]
Hello.
[*He turns to her.*]
I came as soon as I got your call . . .
[*Sadly*]
Arthur, forgive me, I can't do it. You and me, the store;
it's too late. It got too late . . .

ARTHUR
People can change their whole lives if they want to—

NANCY
You just heard that—

ARTHUR
I've been hearing it all day—

NANCY
Arthur, I'm married—

ARTHUR

Oh.

NANCY

I was getting a divorce, that's why I came to the beach
today . . .

ARTHUR

Wherever you get it, I'm delighted—

NANCY

Arthur, I want to go back . . .
[*Crossing to dune.*]
My old buddy, Shirley, I want her back. She didn't expect
a helluva lot, but she didn't shake like this either . . . My
husband's got a used-car lot on Fourteenth Street; nothing'll ever be new there, but I know I'll never be scared
. . . I . . .

ARTHUR

No.

NANCY

Huh?

ARTHUR

[*Quietly, shaking his head.*]
No. You can't go back . . .

[*Comes toward her, at dune.*]

We've gone too far. I built a tree, you built a nose, and we can't go back now . . .

[*He takes her hand.*]

I built that tree today, and while I was doing it I heard this fella laughing . . . laughing with joy . . . and I looked around and it was me. I love you, Nancy. Nancy, Shirley, alla you, I love you and I love my goddamn tree. Please, if your hand trembles, take mine. If you want love, take mine. If you want to love somebody, love me.

[*After a moment*]

Believe me, none of that was easy without a telephone.

[*He touches her cheek.*]

You're beautiful. Forget pretty. Beautiful . . .

NANCY

[*Softly*]

Arthur, it's all new, it's . . .

ARTHUR

No, looks to me like you been beautiful a long, long time . . .

NANCY

Arthur, at night my old nose comes back to haunt the bedroom . . .

[*He carefully pulls the hood of the Mackinaw back off her face.*]

It sniffles and moans all night . . .

[*He holds her face in his hands.*]

It's terrible, you'll hate it . . .

[*He kisses her tenderly. They lean back against the slope of the dune, their arms around each other, the palm tree arched gracefully over them in the moonlight. She talks softly into his shoulder.*]

Arthur . . . Arthur, you figure we got a chance?

ARTHUR

Lady, I learned five chords on the banjo today . . . *anything* is possible.

[*She laughs, she kisses him; holding on to him tightly. They are silent for a moment, lying against the dune, their arms around each other.*]

NANCY

Arthur, God help us, we love each other . . .

ARTHUR

Right . . .

NANCY

We love each other, of all people . . .

[*Silence. They hold each other. Only the sound of the surf.*]

Arthur . . .

[*Silence.*]

Arthur, if you're asleep, I'll kill ya . . .

ARTHUR
Awake, I'm awake . . .
[*He suddenly lifts her up in his arms, celebrating.*]
Awake!

NANCY
Hey, what're ya doin' . . . ?

ARTHUR
Carrying you. I told you, I'm very big on carrying
things . . .

MAX'S VOICE
Put that daughter down! One partner with a coronary is
enough!
[ARTHUR *puts her down, but they continue to hold hands.* MAX
*enters on boardwalk, at left, wearing a red-and-white-striped
blazer and a straw skimmer, his overcoat over his arm. He makes
a small spin, fashion-show style, at the top of the stairs.*]

MAX
And *this* . . . this is why they call it a blazer!
[*Starts daintily down the stairs, continuing the fashion parade.*]
Yessir, and here's Max again . . . this time in smart and
tasty opening-night apparel, he—

NANCY
Max, put your goddamn *coat* on, it's—

MAX

Well . . .
[*Takes note of them holding hands.*]
Looks to me like goodbye Eddie, huh?

NANCY

Pop, I—

MAX

Listen, you want turtle soup, you gotta hurt a couple
turtles, right?
[*Coming down the stairs.*]
Because while we're on the subject of people breaking up
. . . there's certain other news . . .

NANCY

My God, not Mike and Sandra . . .

MAX

No; not Mike and Sandra . . .
[*Picks up crowbar, returning to work at front of store.*]
Max and Rosie.

NANCY

Who?

MAX

Me and your mother, Max and Rosie; in three and a half
weeks we're getting a divorce.

[*Shouting to* ARTHUR.]
   What's with my sign? The organization is getting loose here!
[*Hands the stunned* NANCY *a crowbar.*]
   Come, the boards. Three days! We gotta move here!

NANCY
   Max, you—

MAX
[*As* ARTHUR *takes paint cans from carton.*]
   Get ready with the reds, get ready with the yellows; and I'll give you a tip, gold . . .
[*Begins prying loose one of the boards covering the front of the store.*]
   Nancy, the boards . . .

NANCY
   Pop, I don't believe it . . .

MAX
   Believe it, and then help me with the boards.

NANCY
[*Holding his arm.*]
   Pop, you've been married now for—what is it—forty-three *years*—

MAX
   What can I do, the marriage isn't working out.

NANCY

Pop, forty-three *years, five* children—

MAX

Well, you can't say we didn't try, right?
[*Shouting to* ARTHUR *who works on the sign downstage, near the pier.*]
Silver! Use also silver! For Silverman!

NANCY
[*Draping the overcoat on his shoulders.*]
Max, *why* . . . after all these years, why *now*?

MAX

Because the woman looks funny at me . . .
[*Turns to her.*]
Shirley, the woman looks funny at me. Since I come from the hospital, she looks at me like she misses me . . . and I *didn't leave* yet!
[*Whacks the first board; it falls to the sand. Begins prying second board.*]
These ladies, one little heart attack, they start right away learning to live without you. Trouble is, they learn a little too good and a little too early and all of a sudden you wake up one morning in the same bed with your own widow!
[*Shouting to* ARTHUR, *who has turned from his work to listen to* MAX.]
The sign! What's with the sign? You wanna be known only for your trees?

NANCY
[*Gently*]

Pop . . . Pop, maybe if you talk to her . . .

MAX

Talk to her? Shirley, every morning I come in for break-
fast, the woman is reading the obituaries. I say, "Good
morning, Rosie!" She says, "Guess who died." I say, "Who
died?" She says, "Bing-bing. One minute he was here and
then, bing-bing, he was gone." I say, "*Who*, Rosie, *who*?
Who is Mr. Bing-bing today?" And then she tells me . . .
And, Shirley, I swear to God, *I never heard of him!*

[*Another whack, the second board falls to the sand.*]

For Rosie, anybody who died is automatically a buddy!

[*Puts crowbar down, grips* NANCY'*s arm tensely.*]

Shirley, Shirley . . . in my neighborhood they're gonna
put up soon a lotta new apartment buildings . . . they
paint these big *X*'s on the windows of the old houses
they're gonna rip down . . .

[*He is frightened.*]

Last week we're watching the T.V.; I'm sittin' there in
front of the set like a fish they took all the bones outa,
fillet of person . . . and I catch Rosie lookin' at me . . .
Shirley, she's lookin' at me like she sees *X*'s on my eyes
. . . like she sees 'em painted right on there, like she hears
the wrecking crew coming from blocks away.

[*Shouting to them both.*]

Maybe I'm gonna die, but I guarantee you it's not gonna

be in the middle of the Late Show! Maybe it's the truth
what she sees—but if that's the truth, I don't wanna hang
around with it!

[*Turns sharply to* ARTHUR.]

Gimme that sign!

[*Crosses quickly down to* ARTHUR, *throwing his overcoat off on
the way.*]

The coat! The coat covers my outfit!

[*He grabs the sign from* ARTHUR, *lifts it easily onto his shoulder,
starts up the boardwalk steps with it. The sign is about five feet
by four and does not face the audience at this point.*]

ARTHUR

Max, let me help you with—

NANCY

Pop, damn it, you shouldn't be—

[MAX, *ignoring them both, moves briskly to the top of the stairway and then a few steps along the boardwalk until he is directly
over the store; he lifts the new sign up over the railing, intending
to hook it in place over the old one—he suddenly stops, staggers
. . . He turns away from them and us, grips the railing for support.* NANCY *and* ARTHUR *stand paralyzed for a moment, terri-
fied . . .*]

NANCY

[*Whispering.*]

Oh, my God—

ARTHUR
Max—
[*They both rush forward to the stairs—*MAX *suddenly turns to them, quite calmly, smiling.*]

MAX
Don't make funeral arrangements. I just stopped to take a breath . . .
[*He looks at them both; then looks at* NANCY *for a long moment. Her back is to us; he sees something in her face that we cannot see. He shakes his head.*]
Shirley . . . son-of-a-gun . . . you're lookin' funny at me . . .
[*Quietly, to them both*]
Oh, my sweet children; won't you be shocked . . . my darling children with your frightened eyes, won't you be surprised when I live forever . . .
[*He turns the new sign around, hooks it onto the railing over the old one. The gold and silver letters against a deep-red background are not completely painted in, but still clearly announce: "Max's New Original Hawaiian Ecstasies."* MAX *moves to the side, takes a few steps down the stairs to view the bright new sign above the old store.*]
Twenty-two years, every day, somebody asks me, "What's new?" I say, "Nothing's new." Next week they'll ask; I'll say . . . "*Me.*"
[*Shouting.*]
The sign is up, the sign is up and then the business starts

again . . . look, look, my darling babies . . . soon it begins again . . .

[*His arms raised, shouting, as . . .*

There is a BLACKOUT.

*Immediately in the darkness, we hear the Dixieland Devils, an
eight-piece Dixieland marching band—trumpet, trombone, clarinet, tuba, snare, cymbals, field drum, and marching drum—they
go into a strong and strutting introduction to "Over the Waves."*

*To the beat of this music, light bulbs start to pop on, one at a
time, along the perimeter of the pier. In the light of these first
few bulbs we begin to see more clearly that it is* MAX *who is putting these bulbs in, taking red, yellow, and orange bulbs from his
shopping bag and placing them along the pier; they light up in
time with the music.*

*Toward the end of the intro, there are three downbeats to the
march itself; on the first downbeat, colored footlights go on across
the stage. On the second, the pier lights pulse on brighter; and on
the third,* MAX *marches from the pier to the beach as . . .*

*A sunrise begins in the blackout; a four- or five-minute blos-
soming of light; from gray to pink, from pink to vivid red, and
from red finally to a golden orange . . . In this gradual revelation of light we will see the old stand being transformed into the
new one, all of it done by* MAX, NANCY, *and* ARTHUR *working in
unison. All of their work should be completed when the sunrise
reaches its peak and then—the sky goes night-black, the entire
stage brightly illuminated, amid the dark, deserted beach around it.*

*It is three days later, early evening; all three people are just
completing the last of the tasks we have watched them perform
through the changes of light and time; and there, beautiful and
ugly and glorious, is the New Original Max's Hawaiian Ecstasies.*

The motif is, of course, Hawaiian; the stand appears brightly repainted and it is hung with grass matting, native-hut style; long blades of plastic grass engulf the store, they glisten and rustle in the February wind. The store is framed on either side by two palm trees now, the trunks running up the sides of the building and bursting with enormous palm fronds that dovetail across the roof of the stand; two smaller trees frame the sign above. The counter, hung with fronds and grass, polished and shining, has been outfitted with two new grills, a bubbling tank of coconut drink, and other bright new counter fixtures. The interior of the stand has been decorated with imitation jungle birds, tropical vines, and Tahitian tribal masks. On the sand in front of the store are two round, wicker beach tables surrounded by wicker chairs; umbrellas rise up from the tables, the poles painted like palm bark and the umbrella tops covered with plastic palm fronds. There are colored lights everywhere, the most outstanding light display being a neon frankfurter that forms an archway between the two lampposts on either side of the top of the stairway; each time the frankfurter blinks on and off, it grows smaller, as though bites are being taken out of it—three huge bites; on the fourth bite the frankfurter is gone, and then it reappears whole again. The Dixieland music is coming from a record player on the counter, the record spinning, the music continuing through part of this next scene.

As the lights shift from sunrise to the early evening of this scene, each one of the three people is completing a final task, the music building to a peak . . .

ARTHUR *turns on a glowing red light at the center of a small plaster volcano that he has just placed on the roof of the store.*

NANCY *staples a final large palm frond on the second palm tree.*

MAX *takes a furled banner from inside the store and, half marching, half strutting, carries it to the end of the pier, hooking it onto the tallest of the pier ties, then lets it unroll facing the ocean and the audience; it has silver letters against a blue background and a silver arrow at the bottom; it says: "TO ALL BOATS. STOP HERE FOR MAX'S." At the same moment that the banner unfurls,* ARTHUR *turns on his volcano light and* NANCY *staples the palm frond, their three tasks completed simultaneously.*

MAX *turns from his banner now as the Dixieland music builds to a finish; he looks at the store, at* ARTHUR *and* NANCY. *He takes his hat off to it, to them, and to himself. Then, as if by mutual signal, all three leave their separate positions and rush forward to the center of the beach, where they join in a huge three-person hug.*]

MAX
[*Kissing them both; then squeezing one face with each hand.*]
   I love everything here, each item . . . everything and
   everyone here . . . until further notice.
[*Crossing to coconut drink on counter.*]
   Now the toasts . . .
[*Pours out three drinks in coconut-shell goblets.*]
   I understand '73 is a very good year for coconut drink . . .

NANCY
   Silverman, I'd appreciate it if you'd put on your coat, it's—

MAX
[*Raising his goblet.*]
   To what we did here . . .

[*They all raise their goblets, gathering around one of the wicker tables.*]

To three days that have changed the face of the North Atlantic coastline . . . to Shirley's palm leaves, each a beauty . . . to Arthur's volcano, which I am considering at this moment for a loan-out to the Metropolitan . . . also to Arthur's frankfurter sign, which if I wasn't talking right now would leave me speechless . . . and to Benny Kalsheim . . .

ARTHUR

Benny Kalsheim?

MAX

He come over with me on the boat from Russia, I include him in all toasts.
[*Raising his goblet higher.*]
And to Mr. Marcus Soloway, who comes tonight . . .

ARTHUR

You spoke to him—

MAX

Spoke? Spoke? Sang! We *sang* to each other! A duet! Twin cantors on the telephone!

NANCY

Did he say he'd—

MAX

Soloway don't do business on the phone. He is a person, in person, with a face and no lawyers. He comes to argue, to holler, to hustle; business! I wouldn't miss a minute!

ARTHUR

Yes, but did he say he'd—

MAX
[*Gesturing about with goblet.*]
The truth, partner: do you see a "no" here anywhere? Even a "maybe"?
[*Raising his goblet.*]
To all those present, relatives and associates, lovers and partners . . . and to all Hawaiians everywhere!
[*They clunk glasses and drink.*
Sips thoughtfully.]
Another dash rum, more shreds coconut, we got here easy a dollar-fifty item . . .

ARTHUR

I have a toast . . .
[*They raise their goblets again.*]
To the Silvermans, both of them; and to the sun rising tomorrow on our land . . . the land of Silverman, Soloway, and Korman . . . the blessings of a new day . . . to Coney, island of dreams, island of—

MAX
Wrap it up; we got work here.
[*They clunk goblets and drink.*]
Now you, Shirley, a toast . . .

NANCY
[*She turns to them, raises her goblet.*]
To the store, to the Ecstasies . . . and to the men I love most.

MAX
The best one. She did the best one.
[*They clunk goblets and drink.*]
O.K., party's over!
[*Crossing to phone booth.*]
Tomorrow we open, Soloway comes soon.

ARTHUR
O.K.
[*Clapping his hands.*]
Nancy, Lafayette Electric closes at eight. I've arranged for ten heaters at eighteen-fifty a unit; tell them we'll take a dozen if they come down a dollar each—

NANCY
[*Stacking goblets on counter.*]
A dozen if they come down a dollar, right—

ARTHUR

Velásquez is parked on Stillwell, he'll help you carry them.
[*To* MAX, *who is in booth, dialing*]
Max, when Soloway comes, seat him at Table 2, it's the best view of the area . . .

MAX

Yessir.

ARTHUR
[*Gathering stack of posters and tape.*]
O.K., thirty left, that makes about four hundred posters spread around the—

MAX

Velásquez, he put 'em in the high schools?
[ARTHUR *nods.*]
Good. For the young people, out here will be the in place. Moonlight and coconuts—
[*Into phone*]
Hello, Abrams? Then get me Abrams . . .
[*To* ARTHUR]
The posters, Arthur—Stillwell, Tenth, and don't forget the boardwalk. Soloway should see them whichever way he comes—

ARTHUR

Max, we'll surround him.
[ARTHUR *starts upstairs with posters,* NANCY *heads under boardwalk to street.*]

MAX
[*Shaking the phone.*]
What's with Abrams? I gotta tell him where the parade starts . . .

NANCY
[*About to exit.*]
Parade . . . ?

MAX
Yessir; comes down the avenue at dawn, a fine organization, the Dixieland Devils, to advertise the opening . . .
[*Stands in booth.*]
Rampart Street on Coney Island Avenue! From the land of Dixie, led by Irwin Abrams, what a sound, clean and perfect, everybody struttin' along . . . What, you don't recall those devils? That's them on the record, Shirley; same group when I opened thirty years ago, you marched with me in the parade, you and Michael . . .

NANCY
[*Remembers, smiling.*]
Jesus; they must be very—

MAX
O.K., a tuba died since; also a clarinet; but tomorrow Irwin himself leads, still spunky, a trumpet takes your heart away . . .

[*Gestures with receiver.*]

Takes a little while to get to the phone, otherwise perfect.
[NANCY *and* ARTHUR *enjoying the romance of it as* MAX *rhapsodizes.*]

The selection, naturally, is "Over the Waves"; what could be better? Tomorrow at dawn, windows go up, doors open, everybody looks: "What's that?" A band, eight pieces, a float with a sign "Come to the Ecstasies! On the Beach at Tenth Street!"

[NANCY *blows a kiss to* ARTHUR *and they exit to their tasks.* MAX *speaks into the phone.*]

Hello, Abrams? Silverman! I said *Silverman* . . . That's right, I'm still alive. Yeah, still since yesterday . . . Yesterday, Abrams; I spoke to you yesterday!

[*Shouting into phone.*]

Batteries, Abrams; get new batteries for your machine! *Spend* a dollar . . . Good, it's coming back to you; good, Silverman's parade; you remember. Between the memory and the ears, you're charging too much; how about you come down fifty dollars? . . . Oh, *that* you heard, you heard that one! Abrams, I love you!

[*There is the burst of a match flame on the boardwalk, at left. The flame lingers on the face of* MARCUS SOLOWAY; *lighting his cigar, slowly, elaborately. He is an old man wearing a very new fur-collared ski coat. He blows out the match, steps forward into the light of* ARTHUR's *frankfurter sign at the top of the stairs. He looks up at it, thoughtfully. All this as* MAX *continues on the phone.*]

Abrams, you and the boys, you'll rendezvous with the float

at Surf and Stillwell. Then you'll start down the avenue; you got that? Good, good. And, Abrams, *loud;* you'll play loud! Loud, goodbye!
[*Hangs up; shakes his head.*]
Old people . . .

MARCUS
[*Shouting.*]
Silverman! Soloway is here!

MAX
Soloway!
[*Leaves booth.*]
Soloway!
[*Steps forward to bottom of stairs.*]
Soloway, look at you!

MARCUS
Silverman, look at you! Oh boy, *old*!

MAX
Look at *you*! *Older!*

MARCUS
[*Coming down steps.*]
I heard you was sick.

MAX
They put me in a new ventricle.

MARCUS
Oh boy.

MAX
Dacron.

MARCUS
Oh boy.

MAX
Plastic. Can you believe it?

MARCUS
I believe it. They put me in a pacemaker.

MAX
Oh boy.

MARCUS
Makes me a pace.

MAX
The coat. I like the coat. Sporty.

MARCUS
Thank you. Your coat I don't like. Coats, you never knew.
[*Sits at a table, looking around at store, nodding.*]
Coconuts, you know. But not coats.

[*Pointing at boardwalk.*]
I seen a poster on the boardwalk.

MAX
Good.

MARCUS
A fella is standing next to it; pointing and smiling.

MAX
My partner.

MARCUS
A partner. A pointer and a smiler.

MAX
[*After a moment, indicating the store.*]
Well . . . ?

MARCUS
[*Nods.*]
Nice.
[*Looks about at the lights, the tables; nods.*]
Nice.

MAX
[*Pouring him goblet of coconut drink.*]
Here. Taste.

MARCUS
[*He sips the drink. Reflects on it a moment; then nods.*]
  Nice.

MAX
  Well . . . ?

MARCUS
  Close it up. Max, take the money and close it up.

MAX
  You! From the devil! You're taking money from the devil!

MARCUS
  Why not? I never heard from him before. Twelve thousand dollars; when it comes, I'll take it. At my age, that's
  a good salary; could be a thousand dollars an hour. You
  gather me, Max? You gather my meaning?
[*Leans forward at table.*]
  I come to tell you personally: take the money and close it
  up.

MAX
  Marcus, you won't take the money, you'll join me here . . .
  I got an instinct and a feeling, it's our turn again . . .

MARCUS
  Max, when it was our turn even, it wasn't our turn.

[*Rising from table.*]

Twenty years ago we was flops in July; how come we'll be such winners in February? Take the instinct, take the feeling, take the money, and close it up.

[*Crossing to water's edge.*]

You know what you got here? *Wintertime*. Coldness, Max. And I'm not talkin' in the soul; I'm talkin' in the toes, the nose, and the elbows. Who'll come to shiver with a frankfurter?

[*Turns to him.*]

Even alone, Max; what's the hurry? You can't wait for sunshine?

MAX

A Dacron ventricle don't wait for sunshine.

MARCUS

[*Nods.*]

This is a point.

MAX

[*Comes toward him.*]

You'll come back—

[*Shouting.*]

What's wrong with you? The season is by the doorstep! Every day it gets warmer!

MARCUS

Listen to you! Max, I don't see you now a long time

because you make me nervous! Always excited and you holler too much! Three years ago, the hurricane; I come around here the next day, I'm hoping this place would blow away. The sea should come and get it, it wouldn't aggravate me any more. You gather me? But it didn't blow away and neither do you! You're still around hollering and you make me nervous, Silverman . . .

[*Crosses to* MAX.]

Take my advice, I come to tell you personally: be an old man, you'll live longer . . .

[*Takes his arm.*]

Max, listen to me . . . this year I started doing old-man things. I tell stories for a second time, just like an old man. Sometimes for a third time. It's coming out of my mouth about how I got a good buy on my new car, the third time I'm telling it to my daughter and her husband. I *know* it's the third time, but I go right on, it doesn't bother me; just like an old man. I fall asleep in front of people like it's my right and my privilege, just like an old man. I can remember what I did, what clothes I wore, names of people from when I was eighteen, and if you told me I was in Hong Kong yesterday, I would believe you, because I don't remember; just like an old man. So, I finally figured it out. The reason I'm behaving like an old man . . . is because I'm an *old man*. A *revelation* to me, Silverman; and for the first time in *years* I'm not annoyed with myself. Silverman, I was not a top businessman. I was good, but not first-class. I was an O.K. husband; and as a father, not a knockout. But, Max . . . I'm a *great old man.* I do that the best. I was born for it. I'm seventy-two, Max, and it fits me like a glove. You, you're a crazy. I wish you well with the business; but I can't join you . . .

[*He smiles.*]

See . . . I'm too old for it.

[*He crosses under the boardwalk at right to leave; turns, points to one of the tables.*]

The tables. How much you paid?

MAX

Thirty-eight fifty; Colby's on Fourth Street.

MARCUS

Dumb! Coulda got from Harold's for twenty-five, on Canal Street. You coulda made—

[*He stops himself, turns.*]

Now I'm leaving. Best good wishes to you and yours . . .

[*Crossing into the shadows under the boardwalk at right.*]

Notice how I don't take the stairs. Regard me, how I take the easy way under the boardwalk. I'm seventy-two, Max, and I got one interest in life: seventy-three. You gather me, Silverman . . . ?

[*He exits.*

MAX *looks around at the store for a moment, then shouts in the direction of* MARCUS'*s exit.*]

MAX

The hell with you! A gold mine like this; who needs you

anyway? The coat; I lied to you about the coat. I didn't like it!

[*He nods to himself, satisfied with his outburst. He looks up at the boardwalk, sees an unlit bulb on the string along the railing.*]

A red bulb is out. Leaves a dark spot . . .

[*Rummaging among bulbs in box on the table.*]

Must be no dark spots . . .

[*Finds a red bulb, starts up the stairs with it. He stops about half-way up.*]

How come yesterday twenty-two steps . . . today a thousand?

[*He sits on the top step.*]

ARTHUR'S VOICE

Beautiful . . .

[*He walks into the light of his frankfurter sign at the top of the stairs, carrying the roll of tape, the posters apparently distributed.*]

ARTHUR

Max, you can see this whole place glowin' half a mile away.

MAX

That was the intention.

ARTHUR

[*Coming down the steps.*]

Everything dark, the whole beach, and just this place glowin' like a jewel, Max . . .

MAX

Like a jewel was the intention.

ARTHUR

Neighborhood's covered with those posters, nobody'll be able to walk down a street without—

MAX

Arthur, listen; Soloway was here . . .

ARTHUR

Well . . . ?

MAX

Good news, Arthur. He's selling his share.

ARTHUR
[*Sitting next to him on steps.*]

Doesn't sound like good news, Max . . .

MAX

You gotta have an ear for it . . .
[*Turns to* ARTHUR, *smiling.*]

Arthur, we're rid of him! The man was unfortunately an invalid. A liability to the organization.
[*Taps his chest.*]

A pacemaker in waltz time.
[*Snaps his fingers.*]

Suddenly old.

ARTHUR

Max . . . that means Mister Hot Dog is our partner . . .

MAX

Why not? We open *our* store, we give *them* a percentage, and we don't have an old man hanging around. All we gotta do is show profits by June . . .
[*Holds* ARTHUR's *arm, happily*]
The good news, partner . . . the good news is honor. Honorable battle with Mister Hot Dog. Arthur, if we do good here by June, if we stop *them, that* is a number one victory! A world is covered with plastic and we make a dent! Mister Hot Dog, the nation's number one killer—we're not just keeping a *store* open, it's a public service!
[*He stands.*]
A whistle is blown in the face of the junk parade! Everywhere Mister Hot Dog, but not *here,* Arthur, never *here.*

ARTHUR

[*Rises, goes a few steps down the stairs, looking about at his work.*]
It's really . . . it's so beautiful . . . we've got three months, we've got a chance . . .

MAX

When I pick a partner, I pick a partner!
[*Sits back down on the steps.*]
Poor old Marcus, he lost the eye for paradise . . .

ARTHUR
[*Touching the palm next to the stairs.*]
　　Gotta say so myself, I did a terrific job on these trees . . .
It's the angle of them that does it, I think . . .

MAX
[*Handing him the red bulb.*]
　　Here, there's a light out on the railing . . .
[ARTHUR *takes bulb, going quickly up steps to boardwalk railing.*]
　　Look for the dark spot . . .

ARTHUR
[*As he puts the bulb in*]
　　Listen, did anybody happen to . . . has anybody said anything to you about my trees?

MAX
　　References were made.

ARTHUR
　　Yeah, it's mostly the angle of them that does it. The shape and the angle; I mean, you *know* it's a palm tree . . .

MAX
　　Velásquez brings the tables yesterday, I give you verbatim, he says, "Look what you got here, *palm* trees."

ARTHUR
　　Tell ya what we need, Max.

[*Crossing left, on boardwalk.*]
One more tree, right here . . . right up here . . . something you can see from the street. Whaddya think?
[*No reply.*]
Thing is, I'm gonna have to work out some kinda weatherproof glaze for the plaster; it's—

MAX
Now I can't talk. I'm busy.

ARTHUR
O.K., later; but it's—

MAX
Not later either. I'm busy having a heart attack.

ARTHUR
What . . . ?

MAX
A regular heart attack . . .

ARTHUR
Max—
[*He races across the boardwalk to the steps.*]

MAX
I'll tell you what I'm doing. I'm dying.

ARTHUR
[*Running down the steps, about to go past* MAX *to the phone.*]
 I'll call your doctor—an ambulance—

MAX
[*Grabbing* ARTHUR's *hand.*]
 No-sir. No time. No-sir.

ARTHUR
 Max, the phone, I'll be a second—

MAX
 No-sir—

ARTHUR
[*Kneels next to him on step.*]
 Max, what should I do, I—

MAX
 I don't know. I never died before.

ARTHUR
[*His arm around* MAX.]
 Oh, my God . . .

MAX
 Look at you. If I don't hurry, you'll beat me to it. . .

ARTHUR
 Max, can I . . . can I . . . how do you feel?

MAX

Not in the pink.

[*He stands.*]

Too busy! Who needs this? It's stupid! So stupid!

[*Staggers down the few steps to the sand.*]

I got business. There's business . . .

[ARTHUR *moves down in front of him, trying to hold him.*]

I got business. I got business . . .

He is spent; he falls into ARTHUR's *arms.* ARTHUR *holds him, kneels with him on the sand. There are a few short bursts from a car horn offstage.*]

Arthur . . .

ARTHUR

Yes, Max . . .

MAX

Tell Rosie, say to her . . .

[*He suddenly laughs; a whispered, desperate, delighted laugh.*]

Say to Rosie . . . guess who died.

[*His head falls against* ARTHUR's *chest. He is dead.*

ARTHUR *holds him. There is a gust of wind;* ARTHUR *automatically puts* MAX's *coat collar up to protect him.* NANCY *enters at the top of the steps.*]

NANCY

The heaters are in the car; you'll have to help . . .

[*She sees immediately what has happened. She stands quite still.*

ARTHUR *looks up at her. She begins to nod; slowly, quietly*]
   Sure . . . sure . . .
She comes down the steps, stands near ARTHUR *and* MAX; *she continues to nod, almost hypnotically, whispering.*]
   Sure . . . sure . . .
[*The carnival lights go off; leaving only dim moonlight for a moment, and then there is a . . .*

BLACKOUT

Immediately in the darkness we hear NANCY'S VOICE.]

NANCY'S VOICE
   To all boats. Stop here for Max's . . .
[*During this next speech we will see a gradual change of light lasting the several minutes of her dialogue, the darkened beach turning slowly to bright dawn.*
   In the first beginnings of light we discover NANCY *sitting at the edge of the pier next to the silver and blue banner on the pier tie that reads* "TO ALL BOATS . . ." MAX *is gone, but* ARTHUR *remains seated at the bottom of the steps where we last saw him. The effect is such that* NANCY *has been seated at the edge of the pier all night, speaking through the night till dawn. There are no tears left.*]

NANCY
[*As the dawn lights begin to dim up; she touches the banner.*]
   Sure. The *Queen Mary* was gonna stop here, right? Frankfurters at the captain's table . . . You wanna know who was gonna show up here?

[*Imitating* MAX's *accent.*]

I'll tell you who. Nobody.

[ARTHUR *comes to the end of the pier, stands behind her. She continues, angrily.*]

How dare you, Silverman. How dare you go and die. I paint forty-eight palm leaves and then you . . . Sneaky, sneaky, crazy old man, how dare you die. You hustled me, Silverman; you said you were gonna live forever, and you didn't. So all bets are off, Max. No more crying. I did that last night. That's all you get . . . Am I talking to myself, Max; or am I talking to you? Well, I couldn't tell the difference when you were alive, either.

[ARTHUR *sits next to her; the sunrise grows brighter.*]

This crazy place. He conned us, Arthur. Alive and hollering, he made it look possible: palm trees in February, lovers on sand dunes. But now you are dead, and where are the customers, Max?

[*She closes her eyes, whispering.*]

Listen to the ocean, Arthur; the noise it makes; it roars. If it had an accent I'd think it was him . . . What do I do now? I don't know . . .

[*A blank, wide-eyed stare.*]

Here's me, not knowing. It's my best number . . .

[*The phone rings.*]

ARTHUR

[*Rises, going to phone.*]

That'll be Gallino's; I better cancel the bread order. And

Glickman's Meats, gotta call them also . . .

[*Picks up phone.*]

Hello . . .

[*Quietly; awkwardly*]

Bill; how are ya? . . . Jesus, has it been three days? Sorry about that, I . . . The beach project? Well, it didn't work out very well, no . . . Bill, it's not really funny. Not funny at all . . .

[*There is the sudden sound of an eight-piece Dixieland marching band hitting a loud downbeat, offstage.*]

Jesus . . .

[*The band hits a second downbeat; he turns to* NANCY.]

Jesus, the Dixieland Devils; I forgot to cancel the parade . . .

[*Into phone*]

Hang on a second, Bill; be right back . . .

[*He races up the stairway; as he reaches the top of the stairs the band hits a third downbeat and swings into a strutting, blasting arrangement of "Over the Waves." The offstage music grows gradually louder as the band marches up the unseen avenue parallel to the boardwalk.* ARTHUR, *at the top of the stairs, cups his hands around his mouth and shouts in the direction of the music.*]

Mr. Abrams! Mr. Abrams! Stop! Hey! Mr. Abrams—

[ARTHUR's *hands drop to his sides; he begins to smile.*]

Jesus Christ, that's the oldest bunch of musicians I ever saw . . .

The music grows louder; NANCY *crosses anxiously to the foot of the stairs.*]

NANCY

Arthur, you better go down there and tell them . . .

ARTHUR

Jesus, look at 'em go.

NANCY

Arthur . . .

ARTHUR

They've got this sign . . . it says "Come to the Ecstasies"
. . . all that noise . . . people'll see the sign . . . maybe
they'll . . .

NANCY

Arthur, listen to me . . .

ARTHUR

And there's posters everywhere . . .

NANCY

Arthur, Arthur . . . nobody's gonna come . . .

ARTHUR

Every day it's getting warmer . . .

NANCY
[Shouting above the music.]
Arthur . . . you're not gonna open the store, it's crazy . . .

ARTHUR
[*Shouting down to the open phone.*]
   Hey, Bill! Ya hear that, Bill? That's a parade! Hey, Bill;
got a great idea for our Easter display! How about a bunny
nailed to a cross? By the ears! Ya like that one, Bill? Are
ya laughing, Bill? Just keep laughing, Bill! Goodbye, Bill!
Goodbye! Merry Christmas to all, and to all a good night!
[*Shouting to* NANCY.]
   Hang up the phone!

NANCY
   Arthur—

ARTHUR
   Hang up the phone, Shirley!
[*She hangs up the phone; he turns to look at the parade again,
bouncing with the rhythm.*]
   Boy oh boy, what a class operation . . . Come look, come
on . . .

NANCY
[*Shouting.*]
   Arthur! Listen to me! This place, it's hopeless! It's a monu-
ment to hopelessness!
[*The music reaches a strutting, blasting, swinging peak.*]

ARTHUR
[*Turning to her, smiling.*]

I told you, lady . . . I'm crazy about monuments . . .
[*Shouting above the music.*]
Come on . . . just come and look . . . come see the pa-
rade . . . come on . . . come on . . .
[*Holding his hand down to her, shouting, as . . .*

THE CURTAIN FALLS]